Robert L. Sherbrooke

Speeches and Letters on Reform

Robert L. Sherbrooke

Speeches and Letters on Reform

ISBN/EAN: 9783337295622

Printed in Europe, USA, Canada, Australia, Japan

Cover: Foto ©Suzi / pixelio.de

More available books at **www.hansebooks.com**

SPEECHES AND LETTERS

ON

REFORM;

WITH

A PREFACE.

BY

THE RIGHT HON. R.º LOWE, M.P.

"It is not good to try experiments in states, except the necessity be urgent and the utility evident : and well to beware that it be the reformation that draweth on the change, and not the desire of change that pretendeth the reformation."—BACON.

LONDON:

ROBERT JOHN BUSH, 32, CHARING CROSS, S.W.

1867.

PREFACE.

No assertion is more frequently met with in the speeches of the supporters of a democratic Reform than this,—that the arguments are all on one side, that the question is an easy one, depending merely on arithmetic, and such as any man possessed of ordinary common sense may decide on the first inspection. To me the question appears very difficult to treat in a popular, and, at the same time, in a fair and intelligible way, because it involves not merely the balancing of adverse arguments, but a decision as to what kind of argument should have weight on such a subject. A consideration of the speeches delivered on both sides will show that the arguments in favour of Democracy are mostly metaphysical, resting on considerations prior to, and therefore independent of, experience, appealing to abstract maxims and terms, and treating this peculiarly practical subject as if it were a problem of pure geometry.

The arguments against a democratic change, on the other hand, are all drawn, or profess to be drawn, from considerations purely practical. The one side deals in such terms as right, equality, justice; the other, with the working of institutions, with their faults, with their remedies, with the probable influence which such changes will exert. Are both these methods right, and if not both, which of the two? There are, as a great thinker has taught, three ways of treating political subjects :—the Theological, the Metaphysical, and the Inductive, or experimental. The doctrine of the divine right of kings is an instance of the first kind of treatment of a political subject; the arguments so much relied on at Reform meetings in favour of extended suffrage, and the writings of James and John Mill, are examples of the second; and discussions of the House of Commons on almost every other subject except Reform, and the arguments against Reform, of the third. It is considered, I believe, by most thinkers that the second of these methods is superior to the first, and the third superior to the first and second—so superior as entirely to supersede them, and to afford the only safe guide in political and in many other branches of speculation. I certainly entertain this opinion. When I find a book or a speech appealing to abstract *à priori* principles I put it aside in despair, being well aware that I can learn nothing useful from it. Such works only present to us the

limited and qualified propositions which experience
has established, without their limitations and qualifications, and elevate them into principles by a rash
generalization which strips them of whatever truth
they originally possessed. Thus the words *right* and
equality have a perfectly clear and defined meaning
when applied to the administration of justice under
a settled law, but are really without meaning, except
as vague and inappropriate metaphors, when applied
to the distribution of political power. The proper
answer to a statement, for instance, that all men free
from crime or pauperism have a right to the franchise, is—that this is a question of experience, not of
à priori assumption, and that the assertion, whether
true or false, is inadmissible in political discussion.
But how is this truth to be made evident to a large
multitude when we find men from whom better things
might have been expected, speaking of those who
deny the existence of rights as if they sought to
deprive men of something they really possess, instead
of to explode a vague and meaningless assumption?
The position may be further illustrated by observing,
that if the propositions of this nature which we hear
were true, they would not lead, as they do, to false
conclusions, such as—that men, women, and children,
should have the franchise; that this right applies to
every race in the world ; that this right being prior
to and independent of experience cannot be limited
by experience, and that it is therefore the duty of

a State to do what may be foreseen to lead to immediate ruin in order to satisfy these abstract principles which it has imposed on itself as its guides. The first step, therefore, in the discussion of democratic changes is to clear the mind of these delusive notions, and to employ the teaching of experience, not to qualify or limit, but absolutely to supersede them.

What, then, is the professed object of Reform? It is to improve the structure of the House of Commons. The natural order of investigation is— What are the faults which require correction, and then how will the proposed measures cure those faults? Passion or party spirit may drive men to plunge into the details of a Reform Bill without clearly putting to themselves and answering these questions, but no really conscientious investigator can pass them by unconsidered. In the second of the speeches which this volume contains, I have striven to answer them. I have been charged with optimism, but any one who reads my words will see that I have been exceedingly free in my criticism on the existing House of Commons, not dissembling its blemishes, but seeking to prove that such faults as it has will be aggravated rather than abated by any change in a democratic direction. The weight of this argument seems to be more felt now than it was during the last session, and efforts have been recently made to show that the House has failed in its duty, and that a more democratic Legislature would be more likely to do what is required for the good of the country. To take a few instances. The House, it is said, has not put down electoral corruption, has not diminished pauperism, has not checked intemperance, has not built houses for the poor, has not reduced taxation, has not enforced sanitary arrangements, or given fixity of tenure to Irish tenants, or abolished what is called the monopoly of land. I have no intention to discuss these questions fully in this Preface, but I venture to submit the following considerations.

If every Legislature with which much evil of different kinds co-exists is, on that account, to be condemned and remodelled, I fear that we are passing sentence on free Legislative bodies altogether. It is not for the evils that exist, but for the evils which it is in its power to prevent, that Parliament should be held responsible. Everybody admits this when he judges another in private life, but when we are dealing with public bodies, we cast candour aside, and censure them for things over which they have no control, or which they have done very wisely to let alone. The theory of uneducated or half-educated persons in general is, that Government is almost omnipotent, and that when an evil is not remedied the fault lies in the indolence, the selfishness, or the short-sightedness of Parliament. It is much pleasanter to an audience of non-electors to be told that the franchise would enable them to remedy the evils of

their condition than to be told the real truth, that
the evils they endure are remediable by themselves,
in their individual rather than in their collective
capacity—by their own thrift and self-denial, not
by pressing on Government to do that for them which
they are able, if they will, to do without it. It were
ludicrous, if it were not so sad, to hear speeches
which urge working-men to seek for the franchise, that they may compel Parliament to compel
them to educate their children, or to practise an
involuntary abstinence from intoxicating liquors.
When one man is willing to sell his vote and another
to buy it, what machinery does Parliament possess to
prevent a secret bargain for its purchase? The Ballot
nowhere secures secrecy, and the elections of America
show that in large constituencies bribery is used as
well as in small, especially when parties are evenly
divided. Till Parliament can give health, strength,
providence, and self-control, how can it deal with the
evil of pauperism? If the poor were willing to pay
a rent sufficient to provide them with decent and
healthy dwellings, capital would flow into the business just as it does into the business of building
public houses and gin-shops. With what justice can
Parliament be called upon to tax the community at
large for that which it is in the power of all who receive fair wages to provide for themselves? These
may suffice as specimens of the complaints of neglect
of the interests of the poor which are brought against

Parliament. Parliament does not command boundless resources. A course of the kind indicated would
be felt very sensibly in heavier taxation, and a viola-
tion of sound principles would avenge itself on the
very classes for whose supposed interest they were
violated.

The attempts to enlarge the sphere of Government
action, which the impatience of benevolent persons
urges upon us, can only be made at a heavy sacrifice
of individual liberty. It is said Parliament should
remedy the unequal distribution of land. This can
only be done by curtailing individual liberty of
disposition. That it should give compensation for
improvements to tenants, this can only be done by
invading the freedom of contract. Is it not at least
conceivable that a Legislature which declines to
enter on this retrograde course may be in the right,
and actuated by better motives than prejudice in
favour of one class or antipathy to another?

For my own part, I disclaim such motives. The
end of good government appears to me to be the
good of all, and, if that be not attainable, the good
of the majority; but I must pause when I am told
that the majority, told by the head, should have the
supreme power because they will be sure to do that
which is for their own interest. If this be so, the
solution of all questions is easy indeed. Let us burn
our books, and send round the ballot-box on every
question as it arises? No position can be more

unsound.   If the Queen's Council, as the men of
Kent complained, be no good craftsmen, neither are
good craftsmen necessarily wise councillors. I cannot
blow a glass bottle because it would be my interest
to do so, nor discern political truth merely because
I shall suffer if I am wrong. *Cuique in suâ arte
credendum.* The popular view of the obstacles which
prevent the accomplishment of our wishes for the
happiness of our fellow-creatures is, that there is
a want of good-will in those who have the power
to make laws, while the view which is forced on
every thoughtful man who has practical experience
of human affairs, is, that the real obstacle is most frequently the difficulty of knowing how the end is to be
gained.   The more complicated and artificial society
becomes, and the better we know the principles which
underlie all sound legislation, the more difficult do we
find it to do things which to our ancestors, three hundred years ago, presented no difficulty at all.   Protection, for instance, is the political economy of the
poor, simply because they are not able to follow the
chain of reasoning which demonstrates that they
themselves are sure to be the victims of the waste of
capital which protection implies. I dare say that a
democratic House of Commons would deal with many
of these questions, especially those relating to protection, to the distribution of wealth, and the giving
direct assistance to the poor from the public purse ;
but that does not prove that they would, by doing

so, benefit the poor, or that the interest of the poor
would be promoted by placing in their hands a
more extended power of injuring themselves. From
these considerations, it follows that, of those things
which Parliament is blamed for not doing, many
are impossible, others inexpedient, while some, such
as the regulation of sanitary matters, have actually
been attained without our censors being aware of
it; that what is wanted is not more power to
urge on change, but more intelligence to decide on
what that change ought to be, and therefore that the
standard of intelligence, in constituencies or members,
should on no account be lowered, nor the impulse to
inconsiderate action increased.

Three out of the four speeches which are here re-
printed, were made against a measure which has been
withdrawn. I wish to avoid the discussion of the
issues then raised, but there is one point on which
some explanation may not be out of place. When a
difficult question, on which there is much divergence
of opinion, arises, the first idea of an Englishman is to
find a compromise. Many moderate and liberal men
thought they saw in the Bill of the Government a
moderate proposition in favour of which both extremes might unite. This I have always steadily
denied, not from a wish to drive matters to extremes, but because the nature of the ministerial
measure appeared to make any compromise a capitulation. Neglecting, as unworthy of notice, a large

number of persons, who, though in a superior position
to the 10*l*. householder, have no vote, the Bill enfranchised those below that limit. There was no
principle in the particular amount of rent selected.
It was, as far as it went, purely a concession to numbers. It gave up the present franchise without
providing any stable footing for the future. The
arrangement was a temporary one, and the very same
considerations which caused it would have infallibly
caused a further declension in a few years, with all the
evils of a continual and successful agitation. It may
be said that there is no principle in the present
franchise of 10*l*. and that it is not more stable than 7*l*.
To this there are two answers: in the first place, it
has stood thirty-five years, and been the means of
working many salutary changes. In the second place,
it was established not as a concession to numbers, but
as an alternative to the domination of close corporations. The main principle of the Reform of 1832 was
not the reduction of the franchise. In some boroughs,
Preston for instance, the franchise was raised. The
principle was, to take electoral power out of the hands
of the corporations, which had usurped the property
and the franchise of the borough, and to vest it in the
inhabitants at large. So that the creation of the 10*l*.
franchise was no homage to the principle of numbers,
but a declaration by the statesmen and Parliament of
that day that 10*l*. was at that time, when money was
much more valuable than it is now, sufficiently low

fairly to represent those elements in the borough which deserved representation. To lower 10*l.* to 7*l.*, or 8*l.*, or 6*l.* seems to me a declaration that any limit is of a temporary nature, and must speedily be swept away. That absolute equality is the end, and a periodically decreasing franchise the means. As to the argument that the people have increased in wealth and ought therefore to be admitted to the franchise, it seems to me as cogent as it would be to say, that owing to greater abundance of food the present race of Englishmen had increased in size, and therefore the standard height for recruits ought to be diminished. I have always believed that there is no resting-place in the vertical descent between 10*l.* and household suffrage, and it is because I am opposed to household suffrage, that I am opposed to change in this direction.

Let those who doubt the soundness of this conclusion, consider the following passage from De Tocqueville :—

" When a nation begins to meddle with the elec-
" toral qualification, it may easily be foreseen that,
" sooner or later, it will happen that a qualification
" will be entirely abolished. There is no more in-
" evitable rule which governs society. The wider the
" limits of electoral rights are extended, the more is
" the necessity felt of extending them farther; for
" after each concession the strength of Democracy
" increases, and its demands increase with its new

" power. The ambition of those who are left below
" the required qualification is irritated in proportion
" to the great number of those who are found above
" it. The exception then becomes the rule ; conces-
" sions succeed each other without intermission ; and
" there is no stopping any more until universal suf-
" frage is attained." The fallacy is, that people fix
their eyes on the limited number that is admitted,
and overlook the establishment of principles which
will admit every one.

The problem then is, if we must have Reform,
to find some franchise which shall take in those
above 10*l.* as well as those below, and which,
instead of leading on, by inevitable consequence,
to household suffrage, contains within itself a principle of limitation which may enable it by its own
automatic force to resist the downward pressure which
lurks in the very nature of a money qualification
for a vote. I believe the problem by no means
insoluble.

I may be expected to say a word on the attacks to
which an argument in the second of these speeches,
has been exposed. By what I did say, as opposed to
what I have been misrepresented as saying, I abide.
Did candour form any element in such controversy, it
might have been expected that attention would not
have been limited to a few sentences in speeches
which occupy so many pages. Of the prudence of
what I said I leave others to judge, not concealing

from myself that the verdict has generally on that
issue gone against me. But I would point out that the
working classes, under the modest claim to share in
electoral power, are really asking for the whole of it.
Their claim is to pass from the position of non-electors
to the position of sovereign arbiters in the last resort
of the destinies of the nation. They who set up such
a claim must show that they are masters of themselves
before they can hope to be masters of others. One of
the first qualifications for power should be the willingness to hear both sides—those who say what is un-
pleasing, as well as those who say what is smooth.
They must not seek to limit the field of discussion
by their own susceptibilities. They must expect to
be critically surveyed and canvassed before they
can persuade the present depositaries of power to
abdicate in their favour. If it is competent to me
to argue that with a little self-denial the franchise is
already within the reach of many of them; that they
will swamp the less numerous classes; that the expenses of elections will be increased, and the character
of the House of Commons impaired; it is also competent for me to urge that since corruption and the
other electoral vices prevail most in the lower ranks
of the present constituencies, it is unwise and unsafe
to go lower in search of electoral virtue. It is no
answer to such an argument to abuse its author.
Either the statement is false, in which case it can be
refuted, and will only recoil upon him who made it,

or it is true, in which case it is worthy of the most
serious consideration, not only by the upper classes,
but by the very class which is instructed to resent it,
because that class more than any other will suffer if
Parliament should, through any ill-considered change,
become less fit for the discharge of its duties.

I beg those who may have been induced to think
that I overstepped the fair limits of discussion, to pe-
ruse the following extract from a speech made by Mr.
Bright, at Rochdale, in January, 1859, which contains
some things which I should be very sorry to have said
of the poor, to compare it with the much-censured
passage in my second speech, and then to reflect on a
homely English proverb, which describes the punish-
ment awarded to venial, and the impunity that waits
on grave offences:

" I put it to every man, I don't care what his theo-
" retical notions are, whether he believes that through-
" out the boroughs of the United Kingdom, it would
" be advantageous or beneficial to the constituency as
" a whole, to include some scores in very small con-
" stituencies, some hundreds in others, a few thou-
" sands, perhaps, in the largest, of a class of which
" there are, unfortunately, too many among us, namely,
" the excessively poor—many of them intemperate,
" some of them profligate, some of them, *it may be,*
" only unfortunate, some of them naturally incapable ;
" but all of them in a condition of dependence, such
" as to give no reasonable expectation that they

" would be able to resist the many temptations which " rich and unscrupulous men would offer them at " periods of election—to give their votes in a manner " not only not consistent with their own opinions and " consciences, *if they have any,* but not consistent " with the representation of the town or city in " which they live."

A charge has been repeatedly made against me that I, in a speech made at Kidderminster, in September, 1852, claimed credit with my constituents for having introduced universal suffrage into New South Wales. At that time, the electoral franchise in New South Wales was regulated by the 14th section of the 13th and 14th Vict., which was introduced at my suggestion. By that clause the occupation franchise was lowered from 20*l*. to 10*l*. per annum. The circumstances of the colony rendered, in my judgment, such a reduction in the franchise desirable, in order to keep in check the emancipist class, and to prevent, by a timely concession, the demand for universal suffrage. That clause was re-enacted by Parliament in 1855, and repealed under a power reserved to the local Legislature some two or three years afterwards, for the purpose of introducing universal suffrage. So that I am represented as taking credit for the introduction of universal suffrage, which I did all I could to prevent, at least five years before it was introduced.

The nine months which have passed since the third

of these speeches was made, have afforded ample illustration of what I said of the impatience of democratic
assemblies of any obstacle to their will. In the United
States, the dominant party in Congress settle their
policy in caucus out of the House, and silence the
dissentient minority in the House, by voting the previous question. The President opposes them, and they
proceed to depose the President and diminish the
presidential power. The Supreme Court gives a
judgment adverse to their wishes, and they forth-
with take counsel how they may remodel or destroy
the Supreme Court. Well, may M. Prévost Paradol
say, in the Preface to the fourth volume of his
" Pages d'Histoire :" " *Les progrès de la démocratie*
" *n'ont rien à faire avec les progrès de la liberté, et une*
" *société peut devenir de plus en plus démocratique*
" *sans avoir même l'idée de ce que c'est qu'un État*
" *libre.*"

TO THE INDEPENDENT ELECTORS OF THE BOROUGH OF CALNE.

GENTLEMEN,—I venture to solicit at your hands a renewal of the trust which you confided to me six years ago.

The period which has elapsed since the last general election has been, upon the whole, a time of great material progress and domestic tranquillity. Our material progress I attribute to our steady adherence to, and development of, a sound financial and commercial policy, to our abstinence from foreign wars, and to the unwearied energy and growing intelligence of the nation. Our tranquillity and content I attribute to a well-founded conviction on the part of the people that justice is fairly administered, and the business of Government and Legislation conducted in a spirit of equity and impartiality to all classes of the community.

So long as this shall be the case, I see no reason for great organic changes in institutions which, though partaking largely of the imperfection incident to all things human, and susceptible, doubtless, of great improvements as our experience widens and ripens. have combined order and liberty, stability and progress, in a greater degree than the institutions of any other nation.

Any one who points out a practical evil in the working of our Constitution is entitled to a respectful hearing, and any one who suggests an efficient remedy for such evil shall have my earnest support; but I attach too much importance to the blessings we already enjoy to risk them in pursuit of ideal perfection, or even theoretical improvement.

At the same time, Gentlemen, I believe that the tenure by which we hold our happy constitution is the willingness of the Legislature to inquire into and remedy, without fear or favour, every practical abuse, and its ability to represent fully and faithfully the wishes and feelings of the nation. It was the want of these qualities in the then House of Commons that brought about the Reform of 1832, and I do not doubt that a similar cause would in these times produce a similar result. You will therefore find me, as I have hitherto been, always ready to give my aid to peace, economy, and legal Reform, and to forward to the utmost of my power whatever tends to abolish invidious distinctions and disabilities founded on religious belief.

With many thanks for your former kindness to me, and with the hope that you may find me not unworthy of its continuance,

I am, Gentlemen,

Your faithful and grateful Servant,

ROBERT LOWE.

Lowndes Square, London, June 20, 1865.

MR. LOWE AND HIS CONSTITUENTS.

To THE RIGHT HON. ROBERT LOWE, M.P. FOR THE
BOROUGH OF CALNE.

We, the undersigned Liberal Electors of Calne,
hereby protest against the course you have taken
on the introduction of the Government Franchise
Bill into the House of Commons.

We consider your speech on that occasion to have
been given in utter recklessness of consequences to
the Liberal party and to the Government of Earl
Russell.

You were sent to Parliament to represent this
borough as a Liberal member, and now you are
found running from your allegiance to the Liberal
cause on a vital point, and eliciting, by your animad-
versions on a great Liberal principle, vehement cheers
from the Tory benches.

We have observed with pain and regret the ungenerous and unjust satire you have flung on the
masses of your fellow working countrymen, ignoring

their prudence, self-reliance, and perseverance. Speaking of them, you say, "If you want venality, ignorance, " drunkenness, and the means of intimidation ; if you " want impulsive, unreflecting, violent people, where " would you look ?"

Against this we, sixty-one of your constituents, think it our duty to protest, lest our silence should be held longer to countenance your reaction.

And we have the honour to remain,

JOHN D. BISHOP, and sixty others.

Calne, March 28, 1866.

To MR. JOHN D. BISHOP AND SIXTY OTHER ELECTORS
OF THE BOROUGH OF CALNE.

34, Lowndes Square, April 4, 1866.

GENTLEMEN,—I am very sorry to find that you have felt it your duty to protest against the course which I have taken with regard to the Franchise Bill now before the House of Commons, and that I have not enjoyed the opportunity of offering to you, before you condemn my conduct, the explanation which I now respectfully submit to your candid consideration.

You consider my speech to have been given "in " utter recklessness of consequences to the Liberal " party and to the Government of Lord Russell." By

"recklessness" I understand carelessness or indiffe-
rence, and, so understanding it, I cannot admit the
charge. I view with the greatest concern the divided
state of the Liberal party, and the loss by Lord
Russell of the majority of seventy or eighty which
he inherited from Lord Palmerston, and which might
have been made so efficient an instrument of good
in improving what is defective in the institutions of
the country. The question is—who is to blame for
this? I, who have preferred my principles to my
party, or the Government, who have committed
themselves to such a measure as renders it necessary for many moderate and conscientious. men to
choose between them and the permanent interests
of their country?

You accuse me, after having been "sent to Parlia-
"ment as a Liberal member, of running from my
"allegiance to the Liberal cause on a vital point,"
and thus, as I understand it, convey an imputation
of bad faith on my part towards my constituents.
I submit to you that there is no ground for such an
imputation. On the 3rd of May last I made a speech
in the House of Commons, in which I strenuously
opposed any reduction in the pecuniary amount of
the borough franchise. On the 20th of June last,
in anticipation of the general election, I issued to
you an address, of which the following are extracts:

   " Our tranquillity and content I attribute to a
"well-founded conviction on the part of the people

" that justice is fairly administered, and the business
" of Government and Legislation conducted in the
" spirit of equity and impartiality to all classes of the
" community. So long as this shall be the case, I
" see no reason for great organic changes in institu-
" tions which, although partaking largely of the im-
" perfection incident to all things human, and sus-
" ceptible doubtless of great improvements as our
" experience widens and ripens, have combined order
" and liberty, stability and progress, in a greater
" degree than the institutions of any other nation.
" Any one who points out a practical evil in the
" working of our Constitution is entitled to a respect-
" ful hearing, and any one who suggests an efficient
" remedy for such evil shall have my earnest support.
" But I attach too much importance to the blessings
" we already enjoy to risk them in pursuit of ideal
" perfection, or even theoretical improvement."

　　I expanded the same sentiments in a speech which
I made to you on the day of election, the 12th of
July last. It is therefore, I think, quite clear that I
have dealt with you in the fullest good faith, and
that no elector has any reason to consider himself
overreached or aggrieved by the course which I
have taken with regard to a measure of the very
kind which I distinctly informed you I could not
support.

　　Thirdly, you observe "with pain and regret the
" unjust and ungenerous satire which I have flung on

" the masses of my fellow-countrymen," and you assert
that, speaking of them, I say, " If you want venality,
" ignorance, drunkenness, and the means of intimida-
" tion ; if you want impulsive, unreflecting, violent
" people, where would you look ?" These words are
in the middle of a sentence, the beginning and
end of which have been omitted ; had the passage
been submitted to you in full, I think you would
have seen that it did not refer to the masses of my
working fellow-countrymen at all, but only to practices which notoriously exist in some boroughs among
the poorer class of electors. I was arguing that the
proposed Franchise Bill would increase corruption
and other malpractices at elections, and I put it thus
in substance : " If you find these practices prevail
principally among the poorer class of the present
electors, will you not give a great impulse to them
by lowering the franchise from 10*l.* to 7*l.* ?" The
whole passage, as reported in *The Times*, stands
thus : " *I have had opportunities of knowing some of*
" *the constituencies in this country,* and I ask, if you
" want venality, ignorance, drunkenness, and the
" means of intimidation ; if you want impulsive, unre-
" flecting violent people, where will you go to look for
" them—*to the top or to the bottom ?*"—of what? Of
the constituencies, of course. You will see, by comparing this passage with the portion quoted in the protest
you have signed, that its import is entirely changed
by the omission of the beginning and end, and

instead of being pointed, as it was intended to be, at abuses notoriously existing in many constituencies, and daily exposed before the Election Committees now sitting, it is made to appear as an indiscriminate censure of a whole class, of which I was not speaking. I entirely agree with you, gentlemen, as to the possession by large numbers of the masses of my fellow working countrymen of great prudence, self-reliance, and perseverance, and, indeed, of many other qualities to which we owe the present position of England among the nations of the world. But you will now see that, as I was not, as you suppose, speaking of those masses, I cannot be correctly said to " ignore " these good qualities because I did not mention them. My view has always been, as I expressed it in my speech on the 3rd of May last, that the franchise, as at present established, is a " vast instrument of good, " a lever by which we may hope to elevate the working " classes, requiring a little, and only a little, effort and " self-denial on their part ; a little security that they " are able to conduct their own affairs, before we " intrust them with ours." Since I made that remark, it has been proved by the Government returns that at least a fifth of the borough constituencies is made up of working men. I rejoice at it, and, as a friend of every class in the community, I think it much better that this natural process should be left to work itself out than be artificially accelerated, and should consider it very unfair to the working men who have already achieved this honourable distinction, to mix them up with others who may not have exercised the same prudence and self-denial. Such, gentlemen, are the explanations I have to offer. It would give me great pleasure should I find that they have induced any one of you to reconsider the censure which he has passed upon me.

I am, Gentlemen,

Your obedient humble Servant,

ROBERT LOWE.

MR. LOWE AND THE WORKING CLASSES.

10, Clarendon Gardens, Maida Vale, W.,

Jan. 1, 1867.

Sir,—Believing you will kindly pardon the liberty
I take in thus addressing you, I venture to do so, not
with the presumptuous object of questioning the
views you have seen fit to take on a subject of pro-
found importance to the present interests and future
welfare of this country, but with the more simple one
of asking, in all earnestness and anxiety, if the great
meetings, unprecedented in numbers, order, and enthusiasm, held during the recess, have not induced
you to modify your harsh, unjust, and unfortunate
opinions about the working classes expressed during
the last session of Parliament—opinions which have
tended more than aught else to rouse a spirit of stern,
inflexible resolve, and which, if allowed to foster among
the masses a sense of wrong and insult, may lead to
consequences which few expect and none desire. But
surely you will be ready to confess that the recent
gatherings have been characterized by uniform de-
corum and good conduct, by an entire absence of

drunkenness, violence, turbulence, and the other vices enumerated by you; that on those occasions at least the industrial populations have evinced an honourable eagerness to sacrifice time, means, comfort, and convenience, in a cause which they were sufficiently enlightened to consider sacred and beneficial.

As a member of the Reform League Executive, I should certainly deem it neither wise nor necessary here to indicate the moral to which such imposing and convincing demonstrations of self-control and intelligence appear to me unmistakeably to point; but I do unhesitatingly submit that under these circumstances, if your public utterances have not hitherto been actuated by mere caprice, the moment has arrived when you may well undo what threatens to be a fatal work, and gracefully retract accusations which only enemies of English freedom, English character, and English institutions could hail with pleasure or satisfaction.

Again apologizing for thrusting myself upon your notice, and trespassing upon your time,

I have the honour to remain,

Your obedient humble Servant,

JOSEPH GUEDALLA.

Right Hon. Robert Lowe, M.P.

34, Lowndes Square, Jan. 2, 1867.

SIR,—For many months the Reform League has, by resolutions, handbills, and speeches, accused me of charging the entire working class of this country with venality, drunkenness, and other misconduct. The passage in my speech of March 13, 1866, on which this accusation professes to be grounded, only states that such things do unhappily exist in the constituencies, and that where they do exist they are to be found among the poorer rather than the richer voters. A comparison of these two statements will show— first, that I was speaking of the constituencies, not of the working class at large ; and next, that I only pointed out where such venality and other misconduct as does exist is most likely to be found.

The Reform League having thus fastened upon me assertions which I have not made, has loaded me with the most virulent abuse, and has striven to make me an object of the hatred, perhaps a mark for the vengeance, of my fellow-countrymen.

With such a body and its leaders, of whom you appear to be one, I have no courtesies to interchange. When I think proper to give an opinion on the recent popular demonstrations, it is not to the Reform League that I shall offer it.

You call on me to retract, not what I have said, but your misrepresentation of what I have said.

You can hardly be serious in making such a request. I decline to accede to it, and leave the case to the judgment of the country. I shall send this correspondence to the newspapers.

I am, Sir,

Your obedient Servant,

ROBERT LOWE.

Joseph Guedalla, Esq.

SPEECH UPON THE SECOND READING OF THE BOROUGH FRANCHISE EXTENSION BILL.

May 3, 1865.

In order that I may obtain and merit the indulgence of the House, I shall endeavour to confine myself as much as possible to the exact question at issue in this debate, which is, as I apprehend it, whether it is desirable to extend the franchise in boroughs by lowering its pecuniary amount. That appears to me to be a sufficiently large question for a single speech, without touching any other part of the subject of Reform, because it involves the consideration whether it is or is not expedient, in the existing circumstances of this country, to make a further advance in the direction of democracy. I congratulate the honourable member for Leeds on having to-day succeeded in enlisting the advocacy of the honourable member for Huddersfield in favour of his one-barrelled Reform Bill, although I have no doubt that honourable gentleman would have preferred to handle a revolver. I cannot, however, congratulate the honourable member for Leeds on the arguments in support of his views which the honour-

able member for Huddersfield has advanced. Let the
House for a moment reflect upon what fell from him
towards the close of his speech. He said that if this
Bill were passed it would form an aristocracy among
the working classes, which would be regarded by the
remainder of those classes with jealousy and dislike.
He reminded us of the agency which Trades' Unions
afford ready to the hands of those who would be
animated by this jealousy and dislike to enable them
to extort from this House further reforms. Is the
prospect he thus holds out to us satisfactory? Does
he give us any hope that when this Bill has passed
we shall have settled anything, or does he not make
it quite clear that we shall have unsettled everything?
If I am to judge by this debate, no position is happier
or easier than that of those gentlemen who undertake
to advocate the cause of democracy in the House of
Commons. It is a task which seems to require the
smallest amount of thought and least copious voca-
bulary of words. One honourable gentleman says the
working classes are "wrongfully" excluded from the
exercise of the franchise; another describes their exclusion as "unjust;" a third looks upon them as being
in consequence " degraded ;" while a fourth speaks of
them as being "slaves." So we go on until we have
an accumulation of about a dozen such terms, by the use
of which some honourable gentlemen seem to think
they have done sufficient to prove their case, and to
throw the *onus probandi*—as it is now the fashion to say

—upon those who differ from them in opinion. This extreme facility arises from the fact that the House permits on this subject arguments very different in their nature from those which we are accustomed to expect in dealing with other subjects. Mr. Mill, for instance—a great authority—tells us that his ideal of good government is that every citizen should have a share in it, while the Chancellor of the Exchequer, a still greater authority, says :—

" Is it right, I ask, that in the face of such dis-
" positions the present law of almost entire exclusion
" should prevail?   Again I call upon the adversary to
" show cause, and I venture to say that every man who
" is not presumably incapacitated by some considera-
" tion of personal unfitness or political danger is
" morally entitled to come within the pale of the
" Constitution."

Now, this kind of argument is the easiest in the world, and is widely different from that style of reasoning which the House is in the habit of demanding from its members. Honourable gentlemen will, I think, concur with me in thinking that the true view of the science of government is, that it is not an exact science, that it is not capable of *à priori* demonstration : that it rests upon experiment, and that its conclusions ought to be carefully scanned, modified, and altered so as to be adapted to different states of society, or to the same state of society at different times.   If so, nothing can be more difficult than to meet such concise and

sweeping arguments as those to which I have referred, because a man who is careful to weigh what he
has to say on a subject like this cannot put the results
of an intricate and exhaustive process in a single
sentence. And to what do the arguments of those
who, like the Chancellor of the Exchequer, advocate
the right of the working classes to be admitted to the
exercise of the franchise amount? To that assumption of the *à priori* rights of man which formed the
terror and the ridicule of that grotesque tragedy the
French Revolution. When the Chancellor of the Exchequer said that the *onus probandi* lay with his adversary, in this instance he must have meant that
anterior to the existence of society there was vested
in every man some personal *à priori* right which
nobody had authority to touch. When Mr. Mill, in
like manner, speaks of every citizen of a State having
a perfect right to a share in its government, he appeals
to some *à priori* considerations, in accordance with
which every man would be entitled not only to be well
governed, but to take part in governing himself. But
where are those *à priori* rights to be found? The
answer to that question would lead me into a metaphysical inquiry which I shall not now pursue, con-
tenting myself with saying that I see no proof of
their existence, and that the use of the term arises
from a bungling metaphor, by which a term appropriate to the rights arising under civil society is
transferred to moral considerations antecedent to it.

Can those alleged rights form a ground on which a practical, deliberative assembly like the House of Commons can arrive at a practical conclusion? If they do in reality exist, they are as much the property of the Australian savage and the Hottentot of the Cape as of the educated and refined Englishman. Those who uphold this doctrine must apply it to the lowest as well as to the highest grades of civilisation, claiming for it the same universal, absolute, and unbending force as an axiom of pure mathematics. A man, according to the theory of which I am speaking, derives a right of this kind from God, and if society infringe it, he is entitled to resist that infraction. He is judge without appeal in a cause over which no human tribunal has jurisdiction; he is executioner as well as judge, and so this seemingly harmless dream puts the dagger into the hand of the assassin. Those abstract rights are constantly invoked for the destruction of society and the overthrow of Government, but they never can be successfully invoked as a foundation on which society and Government may securely rest. We heard little of these metaphysical subtleties in 1832, for that generation remembered the controversies which sprung out of the French Revolution; they had the *Anti-Jacobin* by heart, and were conversant with those arguments by which Bentham, the Arch-Radical, the advocate of universal suffrage, had effectually exploded them.

I come to those arguments which may be described

as sentimental. It is contended that it is our business to elevate the working classes, and there is not one of us, I am sure, who would not feel the utmost pleasure in effecting that object. But the way to elevate the working classes is not, it seems to me, to lower the suffrage, the very means of the proposed elevation, or to seek after that sort of elevation which has resulted in Australia in the franchise being so despised that people hardly care to pick it out of the gutter. In Victoria, suffrage is universal. People are registered either in respect of property or person. This last registration must be every three years. In order to raise the franchise and so improve the Government, an Australian statesman hit upon the happy device of requiring a shilling fee for registration. The effect was magical. I am informed that it diminished the personal voters by one-half. A franchise which in the estimation of those who have it is literally not worth a shilling, cannot be a very powerful lever for the elevation of the working classes. Another argument is, that we ought to reward the working classes. This, however, is not a question of patronage; it is a question of selecting the best agency on behalf of a great community to decide in the last resort who are the persons who shall sit in this House, and therefore indirectly what shall be the policy which the British House of Commons is to pursue. It is not a question of sentiment, of rewarding, or punishing, or elevating, but a practical matter of business and statecraft, with

the view to rendering our form of government as
good as possible. It is said, however, that those who
are deprived of the franchise are slaves and degraded.
Now, on this point I should like to read to the House
a few words which appear to me to be extremely
apposite :—

"Many persons do not inquire if a State be well
" administered, if the laws protect property and per-
" sons, if the people are happy? What they require,
" without giving attention to anything else, is politi-
" cal liberty—that is, the most equal distribution of
" political power. Wherever they do not see the
" form of Government to which they are attached,
" they see nothing but slavery, and if these pretended
" slaves are well satisfied with their condition, if they
" do not desire to change it, they despise and insult
" them. In their fanaticism they are always ready to
" stake all the happiness of a nation upon a civil war
" for the sake of transferring power into the hands of
" those whom an invincible ignorance will not permit
" to use it, except for their own destruction."

Where do those words occur? In the *Principles of
Morals and Legislation* of Jeremy Bentham, the advocate of universal suffrage. They seem to me to answer
the question whether in all countries the happiness of
the people at large is not the end which ought to be
sought in the establishment of a Government; and
that end being as far as possible secured, whether we
ought to overthrow the fabric by which it has been

accomplished, on the grounds of sentiment or *à priori* right? I therefore take the liberty of putting aside the sentimental argument, simply observing that the single question is of good government, and not whether by making some change which does not tend to good government, we may do some collateral good to the working or any other class. We should do one thing at a time, and think ourselves very lucky if we do that one thing well. We often hear persons speak of killing two birds with one stone, but I apprehend that the man who tries to do so would be more likely to miss both than to kill either.

There is another argument—the fatalistic argument —which has been put forward by the honourable member for Huddersfield, who has, unintentionally I am sure, done me a great service, for I have constructed for myself a sort of chart or scale of fallacies used on this subject, and he has had the goodness in a single speech to illustrate every one of them. "You must " have it out," the hon. gentleman says, felicitously comparing the constitution of this country to an unsound tooth : "sooner or later you will have to give " way"—using a line of argument which is at once the foundation and the blemish of the great work of De Tocqueville. M. de Tocqueville assumed that democracy was inevitable, and that the question to be considered was, not whether it was good or evil in itself, but how we could best adapt ourselves to it.

This is *ignava ratio*, the coward's argument, by which I hope this House will not be influenced. If this Democracy be a good thing, let us clasp it to our bosoms; if not, there is, I am sure, spirit and feeling enough in this country to prevent us from allowing ourselves to be overawed by any vague presage of this kind, in the belief that the matter has been already decided upon by the fates and destinies in some dark tribunal in which they sit together to regulate the future of nations. The destiny of every Englishman is in his own heart, the destiny of England is in the great heart of England, and to that, and not to dreams and omens, I look as the arbiter of her fate.

I come next to the argument of necessity. We are told that the working classes are thundering at our gates, and that we shall be in the greatest danger if we do not accede to their demands. But when, in answer to this argument, it is suggested that they are not at our gates, and that they are making no noise, the reply is, " Oh, wait awhile and see what they will " do." Now, I, for one, am disposed to take that advice, and to wait awhile. If this which we are asked for be a good thing in itself to concede, let us grant it without any compulsion ; but if it be bad, let us not be driven from our sense of manliness and duty to our country by any fear as to what may happen if we refuse it. I am inclined to think that Democracy in the present state of things would be a great misfortune. If driven to it, we must, of course, submit, and it may perhaps be better to do so than to give rise to a great internal commotion or civil war; but it will take a very severe compulsion to induce me to counsel suicide. The advice to yield at once, lest a worse thing befall us, reminds me of the lines—

> " He thought with a smile upon England the while,
>   And the trick that her statesmen had taught her,
> Of saving herself from the storm above,
>   By putting her head under water."

I have now gone through a series of arguments to which, in my opinion, the House ought not to attach any weight. To what kind of arguments, then, do I think they ought to listen ? I will not state them in my own language, but in the language of one the poetical charm of whose mind and style have perhaps a little overclouded his reputation as a political philosopher. I allude to Lord Macaulay, and these are his words :—

" How then are we to arrive at just conclusions on " a subject so important to the happiness of man- " kind? Surely by that method which, in every " experimental science in which it has been applied, " has signally increased the power and knowledge of " our species, by observing the present state of the " world, by assiduously studying the history of past " ages, by sifting the evidence of facts, by carefully " combining and contrasting those which are authentic, " by generalising with judgment and diffidence, by

" perpetually bringing the theory which we have
" constructed to the tests of new facts, by correcting
" or altogether abandoning it, according as those new
" facts prove it to be partially or fundamentally
" unsound. Proceeding thus — patiently, diligently,
" candidly—we may hope to form a system as far
" inferior in pretension to that which we have been
" examining, and as far superior to it in real utility
" as the prescriptions of a great physician, varying
" with every stage of every malady and with the consti-
" tution of every patient, to the pill of the advertising
" quack which is to cure all human beings, in all
" climates, of all diseases."

That, I humbly submit, is the way in which you
must look at this question. You must deal with it
as practical men, upon grounds and for reasons of
which I have scarcely observed a vestige in this debate. What should be the nature of your previous
inquiries into the subject, I shall now venture to point
out. To use the words of one whose name ought
never to be mentioned in this house without respect,
if not with a warmer feeling—the late Sir G. Lewis—
I might say that what we have to do is to find out
any practical evil in the working of our institutions,
and then to suggest a remedy for it. We ought
always to be ready to listen. The inductive method
abhors dogmatism, and therefore excludes finality.
Its ears are always open to new facts. It re-
cognises knowledge as perpetually advancing. It

rejects no new light. It leaves overweening confidence to *à priori* reasoners, sentimentalists, and
fatalists. It is a safe because a modest guide. No
one has, however, in this instance shown a single
practical grievance under which the working classes
are suffering which would be remedied by the proposed alteration. Mr. Holyoake, speaking on behalf
of those classes, tells us that the Frenchman who has
voted away his own liberty is far superior to the
Englishman who possesses his liberty, but does not
possess the franchise. I think we have a right to
ask for even a more tangible grievance from the
working classes than the absence of the power to ruin
themselves. Having thus shown what kind of arguments we ought and ought not to receive, I think I
may confidently assert, in opposition to the Chancellor
of the Exchequer, that the *onus probandi* in this case
rests not with those who deny the existence of the
à priori right for which he contends, but rather on
those who, unable to point out the existence of any
practical grievance, call upon us virtually to destroy
our present form of Government and to put something else in its place. It may be said, however, that
a practical grievance does exist, and that the interests
of the working classes are not consulted by the House
of Commons ; but, in answer to that argument, I
would simply refer to the admirable speech of the noble
lord the member for Haddingtonshire, and remark
that honourable gentlemen frequently bring forward

questions which really relate to rich bodies, as if they
were connected with the poor, convinced that by such
means they will secure for their applications a greater
degree of sympathy. I entirely deny that the interests of the poor are neglected in this House. I
maintain that legislation is not altogether a matter of
good-will, as in the small republics of Greece, the
study of whose municipal squabbles is the occupation
of our boyhood, but of intelligence and study, and
that the abstruse problems which it involves cannot
be satisfactorily dealt with by men at that time engaged in daily labour. In 1842, the late Mr. Dun-
combe presented a petition to this House signed by
3,000,000 persons. This petition may, therefore, I
think, be looked upon as containing a fair expression
of the views of the working classes, whose political
views must be toned down to the comprehension of
persons, and in it they say :—

"Your petitioners complain that they are enor-
"mously taxed to pay the interest of what is called
"the National Debt, a debt amounting at present to
"800,000,000l., being only a portion of the enormous
"amount expended in cruel and expensive wars for
"the suppression of all liberty by men not authorized
"by the people, and who, consequently, had no right
"to tax posterity for the outrages committed by them
"upon mankind."

There goes the National Debt. "Your petitioners
"deeply deplore the existence of any kind of mono-

" poly in this nation; and while they unequivocally
" condemn the levying of any tax upon the neces-
" saries of life and upon those articles principally
" required by the labouring classes, they are also
" sensible that the abolition of any one monopoly
" will never unshackle labour from its misery until
" the people possess that power under which all
" monopoly and oppression must cease. And your
" petitioners respectfully mention the existing mono-
" polies of the suffrage "—pointing, of course, to
universal suffrage—" of paper-money "—looking naturally to unlimited issues and greenbacks—" of ma-
" chinery "—meaning property, because machinery is
only one kind of property—" of land "—of course
there could be no question about that—" of the
" public press "—such portion of it as was opposed
to their views—" of religion, of the means of travel-
" ling and transit, and a host of other evils too
" numerous to mention, all arising from class legis-
" lation." That was the working men's programme
of the steps which Parliament ought to take for the
regeneration of the country and the advancement of
the class to which they belonged. The middle-class
Parliament, if I may call it so, did not adopt that
programme. It took another course. It struck off
the shackles from trade, meeting while doing so with
every possible opposition from the working classes,
who, organized by their leaders, did everything they
could to break up the meetings of persons engaged in

forwarding this beneficial policy. And it founded a system of education which, though no doubt imperfect, has been an enormous boon to the working classes. If the working classes had had their way then instead of the middle class having had theirs, by which course of action would the working classes most have benefited? Would it have been a gain to them to obtain control over the affairs of the country? I do not speak of monopolists like ourselves, who, of course, would have disappeared off the face of the earth, but of the working classes themselves—would they have gained by the attainment of their own wishes?

> " Evertere domos totos optantibus ipsis
> Dî faciles."

I venture to think they would not have gained by it, and that the working classes, instead of being neglected by the existing Parliament, have been better cared for, and according to sounder and more carefully considered principles, than if they themselves had been charged with the administration.

These are the reasons that appear to me to show that no satisfactory grounds have been laid which should induce the House to read this Bill a second time. And now I go a little farther, and, thanking the House for the patience with which they have listened to an abstract and distasteful discussion, I propose to take on myself the burden of showing that the Bill ought not to pass. The first thing that strikes me is that this Bill will give the franchise to very few of the working classes in whose power it is not to obtain it now. And on that point I beg leave to read a passage from the report of the Factory Commissioners for the present year, which seems to me very interesting and suggestive. One of the inspectors, Mr. Baker, speaking of a freehold land society that has been eminently prosperous, says :—

" The simple fact of these savings being effected,
" and of these houses being erected, by the will of
" working men, is an immensely significant one. All
" these owners of houses are freeholders, and every
" man has earned his own freehold from a desire to
" possess it. While in the same locality, employed
" at the same work and the same wages, and without
" any extraordinary drawback, a vast number of those
" who possess no such properties live on from day to
" day, regardless of every enjoyment which is not
" sensual, exhibiting no desire for an elevation of
" character among their fellow-men, wasting their
" money in profitless pursuits, or in degrading
" pastimes, and being for ever unprepared for the
" commonest vicissitudes which bring such misery in
" their train."

I ask the House upon which of the classes here described will the Bill of the honourable member for Leeds operate ? Not upon the provident, but mainly upon the improvident class. For the provident are not only in possession of the franchise—they have soared

far above it, and have got into the region of freeholders. It will, therefore, apply to the men who
waste their time in these profitless and degrading
pursuits, in order that they may be elevated and
fished out of the mire in which they delight to grovel,
introduced to power, and intrusted with control over
the Constitution of the country. Not to take an
extreme case, the Chancellor of the Exchequer says
that 600 quarts of beer is a fair average consumption
for every adult male in the course of the year, and,
taking beer at 4d. a pot, the consumption of 240
quarts represents an annual outlay of 4l. If, therefore, persons who live in 8l. houses would only forego
120 quarts annually, they might at once occupy a
10l. house, and acquire the franchise. That is the
exact measure of the sacrifice which is required on
their part to obtain this much-coveted right, to raise
themselves from the position of slaves, to wipe off
from their characters the mark of degradation and all
the other horrors that have been so feelingly depicted.
That is by no means all. I have no wish to demand
from the working man any great amount of rigid
self-denial. I am neither an ascetic in theory or
practice. But I would point out that there is a
certain amount of accommodation, especially of sleeping accommodation, which is absolutely necessary
for the preservation of the commonest decency and
morality, for the avoidance of the most frightful im-
purities and even crimes. The amount which it is

necessary to expend in rent for these purposes, and the preservation of the health of the poor man and his family, will, with a very slight addition, infallibly obtain for him the franchise. And the question for you now to determine is, whether you ought to bring down the franchise to the level of those persons who have no such sense of decency or morality, and of what is due to the health of themselves and their children—whether you will degrade the franchise into the dirt, and imperil your institutions — or whether you will make this franchise a vast instru- ment of good, a lever by which you may hope to elevate the working classes—not in the manner which a mawkish sentimentality contemplates, but by fixing the franchise at a reasonable level, requiring a little, and only a little, effort and self-denial on their part, a little security that they are able to conduct their own affairs before we entrust them with ours ?

Another objection which I have to the Bill refers to its swamping aspect. I have made an analysis of the figures presented to us in 1860—for we have no later—and I find that the effect of this Bill, which is described as harmless and innocent, would be in five large towns to treble, and in twenty-eight large towns to double, the constituencies. Now I ask honourable members, when the present constituency is doubled or trebled by an Act of this House, what becomes of the present constituency ? *Quid superest de corporibus ?* You might as well abolish it altogether. Not only is

it increased—it is diluted; and the additions being
all of persons rated below 10*l.*, these have a sort of
chemical affinity with persons of the same class
a little above themselves, and the two united
become masters of the situation. In these cases,
therefore, the present constituency, including all the
property and all the intelligence of the place, would
be disfranchised without a prospect of escape; and
this, I venture to think, would be a very great evil.
The noble lord, the member for Haddingtonshire, has
truly said that many people want something in the way
of change; but that something is anything in the world
but what this Bill proposes. They want universal suffrage; they want an educational franchise; they want
a provident franchise; but nobody wants a 6*l.* franchise. I know not whether that was the intention, but
it seemed to me that the speeches in support of the
Bill, especially the speech of the honourable member
for Huddersfield, go direct to universal suffrage. Can
you believe that this thing, which nobody wants, will
be accepted as anything but a step to universal suffrage,
or that it is likely to form in any way a permanent
settlement of the question? It is assumed by every
speaker in favour of the Bill, that when it passes the
matter will be settled for ever, and that we shall be
freed from those terrible visions of pressure from
without which are always conjured up and brought in
aid of the argument. But is that so? If you cannot
maintain a 10*l.* franchise, how can you hope to make

a stand at 6*l.*?   Look at the prestige surrounding this
10*l.* franchise, created when the country was in the
highest state of discontent.   I can remember the time
myself when the House of Commons was regarded, not
as representing the wishes and forwarding the views of
the bulk of the English people, but as the greatest obstacle in the way of carrying out improvements which
were desired by them.   And that was not merely the
opinion of the working classes; it was an opinion shared
to a great extent by the education and property of the
country, and but for which conviction the Reform Bill
never would have passed into law.   Let me ask, have
not the results fulfilled and exceeded the expectations
of the most sanguine prophet of that time?   Look at
the noble work, the heroic work, which the House of
Commons has performed within these thirty-five years.
It has gone through and revised every institution of the
country ; it has scanned our trade, our colonies, our
laws, and our municipal institutions ; everything that
was complained of, everything that had grown distasteful, has been touched with success and moderation by the amending hand.   And to such a point
have these amendments been carried, that when gentlemen come to argue this question and do all in their
power to get up a practical grievance, they fail in sug-
gesting even one.   The 10*l.* franchise, if not the most
venerable, is at any rate one of the most respectable
institutions that any country ever possessed.   The seven
Houses of Commons that have sat since the Reform

Bill, have performed exploits unrivalled, not merely in
the six centuries during which Parliament has existed,
but in the whole history of representative assemblies.
With all this continued peace, contentment, happiness,
and prosperity, if the 10l. franchise cannot maintain
itself against such speeches as we have heard to-day,
what chance have we of maintaining any other franchise whatever? It is simply ridiculous to suppose
that we can do so.   The thing is fated from the moment that the House, abandoning a position which
should never be yielded while hope remains, consents
to take up another not one-hundredth part as strong, on
the road to universal suffrage.   It is trifling with the
House to suggest that when you have passed this Bill
you have settled anything ; all that you do is to un-
settle everything, perhaps to lay the foundation of a
real agitation, because people, when they find that so
much can be gained with such little trouble, will be
encouraged to ask for a good deal more.

Two answers have been suggested to this view.   It
is said that the working classes will not act together.
Assertions are very cheap on such subjects, but look
at the probabilities. If you have a large infusion of
voters from the working classes, they will speedily become the most numerous class in every constituency.
They therefore have in their hands the power, if they
only know how to use it, of becoming masters of the
situation, all the other classes being, of necessity,
powerless in their hands. Is it possible to suppose

that in the present state of society, with the widely-
conducted operations of the press, and public discussions on every subject, the working classes can long
remain in ignorance of their power? You cannot treat
them like pigs or cattle, or like Curran's fleas, " which,
" if they had been unanimous, would have pulled him
" out of bed." You know very well that they will soon
possess the secret of their own power, and then what
is to prevent them from using it ? What are the re-
straints that you propose ? I know that very pretty
metaphors have been given us ; we were told, for instance, that society is divided into vertical instead of
horizontal strata, but nevertheless, when men have
power conferred on them, infallibly they will employ
it for their own purposes. Are we without information
to guide us in the matter ? Have we not examples
before our eyes? Look at Australia. There, universal
suffrage was conceded suddenly, and the working
classes, immediately availing themselves of it, became
masters of the situation. Nobody else has a shadow
of power. Does anybody doubt that in America the
working classes are the masters ? Why, there is the
greatest apathy among the upper classes, because,
though not actually disfranchised, we know that virtually they are so by reason of the supremacy of numbers that weighs them down. And why should it be
otherwise in England ? It appears to me that nothing
can be more manifest, looking to the peculiar nature
of the working classes, than in passing a Bill such as is

now proposed you take away the principal power from property and intellect, and give it to the multitude who live on weekly wages.

I am sure the House will agree with me that it is an observation, true of human nature as of other things, that aggregation and crystallization are strong just in proportion as the molecules are minute. It is the consciousness of individual weakness that makes persons aggregate together, and nowhere is that impulse so strong as in the lowest classes of society. Nothing is so remarkable among the working classes of England as their intense tendency to associate and organize themselves. They have done so for the purpose of establishing benefit clubs, and to make provision for sickness and old age. These associations once existing for praiseworthy objects, one might suppose that they would end there. But no. Once having established the principle of association, this has been used for very different purposes. The working classes select leaders—by no means the best or wisest among them—and to those men they submit with a docility which would be admirable were it not perpetuated and enforced by the reign of terror kept up among and by themselves. I shall not refer to the subject of strikes; but it is, I contend, impossible to believe that the same machinery which is at present brought into play in connection with strikes would not be applied by the working classes to political purposes. Once give the men votes, and the machinery is ready to launch those votes in one compact mass upon the institutions and property of this country. It is so in America. The wire-pullers and log-rollers there correspond exactly to the leaders whom the working classes follow in the matter of strikes at home. These leaders may be, probably are, men little known ; apparently very retiring and insignificant, but nevertheless they wield the masses with the greatest ease. The elector, perhaps, does not know the name of the candidate for whom his vote is to be recorded. Papers for the election of every one, from a governor down to a constable and up again to a member of the Congress, are handed to him in a bundle, tied round with a dirty piece of string, and the elector votes in the sense required—I have often seen it done—because his Mr. Potter or his Mr. Odgers desires him to do so.

It is said, " Oh, but though we are to have an in-" crease of democratic power, we shall also have safe-"guards," and Mr. Mill and Lord Grey, the philosopher and the statesman, have busied themselves in inventing these safeguards. I can fancy no employment more worthy of the philosopher and statesman than the invention of safeguards against democracy, but I can fancy no employment less worthy of either statesman or philosopher than counselling us to give a loose rein to democracy in order that we may see whether we cannot get back what we have given in another way. It may be very wise to throw 100*l.* out of the window to a mob, it may be very right to give largess in that manner ; but it is the height of folly to throw out the 100*l.* in the hope and expectation that the mob will bring it back again to you in detail, sovereign by sovereign. Besides, consider how this is trifling with a great question. If we make these concessions to the spirit of Democracy, if we give facilities for getting rid of some of those monopolies to which I referred just now, are the gentlemen who lead the Democratic party, are the persons who make up the mass of that party, so silly as to allow themselves to be tricked out of the fruits of their victory by a few transparent dodges, so clear that they would not deceive a child ? The question is, are we making such concessions as are required to meet any practical grievance ? That we ought to do and no more ; if we make more in the hope of getting them back again, we shall be allowing the fish to run away with the line, which we shall never be able to wind up again. I think I have shown the House that it is neither wise nor safe to rely on the measure before us.

The only practical mode of dealing with this question, in a manner worthy at once the dignity of this House and the character of the English people, is to guide our course by the light of experience, gained from what has been done in former times—above all, in our own country, the great nurse of freedom and of the happiness of the whole human family. I have shown you that the Bill of the honourable member for Leeds, while it satisfies nobody, will cast us loose from our only safe moorings in the 10*l.* franchise, and set us adrift on the ocean of Democracy without chart or compass ; and I think I have also shown you that, as it is ridiculous to expect the working classes, once in possession of absolute power, would refrain from using that power, the British Constitution ought never to exist upon sufferance. I am not going to inflict on the House an essay on the British Constitution, but this I will say, that it is the most complicated, probably, that the world ever saw. The number and variety of interests, and the manner in which these are entwined with each other, serve to make up a most curious piece of mechanism, but, in practice, well confirm the precept which Aristotle laid down 2000 years ago in the words—" Happy and well governed those States " where the middle part is strong and the extremes " weak." That description well embodies the leading merit of our Constitution. Are we prepared to do away with a system of such tried and tested efficiency as no other country was ever happy enough to possess since the world was a world, and to substitute for it a form of government of extreme simplicity, whose tendencies and peculiarities have been as carefully noted and recorded as those of any animal or vegetable, with whose real nature we have no excuse for not being well acquainted—pure Democracy ?

I am no proscriber of Democracy. In America it answers its purpose very well ; in States like those of Greece it may have been desirable ; but for England,

in its present state of development and civilization, to
make a step in the direction of Democracy appears to
me the strangest and wildest proposition that was
ever broached by man.   The good government which
America enjoys under her Democracy—whatever estimate honourable gentlemen may be disposed to
form of it—is absolutely unattainable by England
under a Democracy, and for this reason :—America,
in her boundless and fertile lands, has a resource
which removes and carries off all the peccant political
humours of the body politic.   Turbulent demagogues
out there become contented cultivators of the land ;
there are no questions between landlord and tenant ;
every one can hold land in fee simple if he chooses,
and transmit it to his children.   The wealth which
America possesses is of a kind which her people did
not make, and which they cannot destroy ; it is due
to the boundless beneficence of the Giver, beside
whose works those undertaken and executed by the
human race sink into insignificance. The valleys even
of the Nile, the Tigris, and the Euphrates, seem
ridiculously small when compared with the valley of
the Mississippi, which it has been calculated would
afford residence to 240,000,000 of people without over-
crowding.   No tumult, no sedition, can ever destroy
these natural advantages.   But what is our property
here ?   It is the fabric of the labour of generations,
raised slowly and with infinite toil, and to continue it is
indispensable that it should rest on secure foundations.

Look at the land question alone. In America nobody covets land, because he can get as much as he likes there for less money than would represent the trouble of kicking anybody else out of his holding. But here the case is different; nothing is easier than to get up a cry about land, and at this moment it is believed all over the Continent that there is actually a law in existence under which the possession of the land of England is confined exclusively to the aristocracy. Our prosperity rests more than anything else in the world upon our credit. What sort of credit should we maintain had we a Government like that of America, where the rate of interest at which their national debt has been raised is such that they will pay more for a debt of 500,000,000*l.* than we do for a debt of 800,000,000*l.*? Once introduce the American system of government here, and the mighty fabric of English prosperity would, I am satisfied, vanish like an exhalation. And now I do solemnly ask the Liberal party to pass in review their own position with regard to this question. They have to make their choice not merely on the fate which shall befall this particular Bill, but with the full knowledge that a general election is to follow. And I ask whether it is to go forth that the party of liberality and progress in this country does or does not for the future cast in its lot and identify its fortunes with that particular form of government called Democracy, which has never yet been the government of this country.

It is a momentous issue which we have to try; and nothing but a sense of its enormous importance induces me to do what the House will believe is not a pleasant duty—to make my present speech in the neighbourhood in which I stand. I view this, however, as a question between progress and retrogression. So far from believing that Democracy would aid the progress of the State, I am satisfied it would impede it. Its political economy is not that of Adam Smith, and its theories widely differ from those which the intelligent and clear-headed working man would adopt, did his daily avocation give him leisure to instruct himself. It is always introducing an ungrateful subject to make personal references, but perhaps I may be allowed for a moment to quote myself. Gentlemen think it the height of illiberality on my part, and believe that I am abandoning the cause of progress, because on this occasion I refuse to follow their steps. Of course, I was quite prepared for that; but nevertheless I have been a Liberal all my life. I was a Liberal at a time and in places where it was not so easy to make professions of Liberalism as in the present day; I suffered for my Liberal principles, but I did so gladly, because I had confidence in them, and because I never had occasion to recall a single conviction which I had deliberately arrived at. I have had the great happiness to see almost everything done by the decisions of this House that I thought should be carried into effect, and I have full confidence in the progress of society to a degree incalculable to us; my mind is so constituted as to rely much on abstract principles, and I believe that by their application the happiness and prosperity of mankind may be enormously augmented. But for the very reason that I look forward to and hope for this amelioration—because I am a Liberal, and know that by pure and clear intelligence alone can the cause of true progress be promoted, I regard as one of the greatest dangers with which the country can be threatened a proposal to subvert the existing order of things, and to transfer power from the hands of property and intelligence, and to place it in the hands of men whose whole life is necessarily occupied in daily struggles for existence.

I earnestly hope—and it is the object I have in view—that I may have done something to make men think on this question—to pick it out of the slough of despond in which it has wallowed. Sir, I have been weary and sickened at the way in which this question has been dealt with. The way in which the two parties have tossed this question from one to the other reminds me of nothing so much as a young lady and young gentleman playing at battledore and shuttlecock. After tossing the shuttlecock from one to the other a few times, they let it drop and begin to flirt. The great Liberal party may well be presumed to know its own business better than I do. I venture, however, to make this prediction—that if they do unite their fortunes with the fortunes of Democracy, as it is proposed they should do in the case of this measure, they will not miss one of two things—if they fail in carrying this measure they will ruin their party, and if they succeed in carrying this measure they will ruin their country.

SPEECH ON THE REPRESENTATION OF THE PEOPLE BILL.

FIRST READING. ADJOURNED DEBATE.

13th March, 1866.

SIR, in the course of a long and illustrious career, this House of Commons has gathered into its hands a very large proportion of the political power of the country. It has outlived the influence of the Crown; it has shaken off the dictation of the aristocracy; in finance and taxation it is supreme; it has a very large share in legislation; it can control and unmake, and sometimes nearly make, the executive Government. Probably, when the time shall arrive that the history of this nation shall be written as the history of that which has passed away, it may be thought that too much power and too much influence were concentrated and condensed in this great Assembly, and that England put too much to hazard on the personal qualifications of those who sit within these walls. But, Sir, in proportion as the powers of the House of Commons are great and paramount, so does the exploit of endeavouring to amend its constitution become one of the highest and noblest efforts of statesmanship. To tamper with it lightly, to deal with it with unskilled hands, is one of the most signal acts of presumption or folly. When we speak of a Reform Bill, when we speak of giving the franchise to a class which has it not—of transferring the electoral power from one place to another, we should always bear in mind that the end we ought to have in view is not the class which receives the franchise, not the district that obtains the power of sending members to Parliament, but that Parliament itself in which those members are to sit, and for the sake of constituting which properly those powers ought alone to be exercised. To consider the franchise as an end in itself—to suppose that we should confer it on any one class of persons because we think them deserving, that we should take it away from one place because it is small, or give it to another because it happens to be large, is, in my opinion, to mistake the means for the end. The franchise is an enormous advantage to this country—we are naturally enamoured of it; but when we look upon it in the light which I have just mentioned, and regard the conferring of it as the ultimate effort of statesmanship, as a matter of Reform, we, it appears to me, fall into the same error as the man would do who, having found that money had contributed much to his pleasure when young, and to his power in middle life, should, when he was

approaching the close of his days—when pleasure
could charm him no more, and power was no longer
within his grasp—turn his attention from the end to
the means, and terminate by loving money for its
own sake. I mention this because I have, I think,
some right to complain of my right honourable friend
the Chancellor of the Exchequer for the manner in
which he introduced the great subject under discussion to the notice of the House. The Chancellor of
the Exchequer told us, in substance, that he feared
he had much to say to the House, and that he would
not, therefore, take up our time by entering into the
arguments or reasons in favour of a revision of our
electoral system, or the extension of the electoral
franchise. Now, Sir, I wish to speak on this matter
with perfect temper and good humour; but I cannot
help believing that my right honourable friend will
be of opinion that in taking the course I have just
mentioned he did not deal altogether respectfully
with the House. It is not right that a great Assembly
like this should be called upon to entertain a proposition of the very utmost moment, touching most
nearly a most vital part of our Constitution—effecting,
in fact, if carried into law, an immense re-distribution
of political power and an enormous alteration in the
constituencies of the country—it is not right, I say,
that such a proposition should be introduced to us,
without having the reasons which induced the Government to lay such a proposition before us stated by the

F

Minister by whom it is introduced, so that we may have something to guide us in estimating his scheme and the principles upon which it is based. For my own part, I am not very particularly wedded to anything just because it exists, and I am quite prepared to follow experience and expediency as my guide in political matters wherever they may lead me. I have no prejudice in favour of the existing state of things. I care not, as far as any feelings or prejudices of my own are concerned, what the amount of the franchise is, or what the place in which Parliamentary power is vested. These are questions I am free to consider, because I wish to be guided by experience and induction, which, from their very nature, are always open to new light, from whatever quarter it may come, and by which everything is repudiated which savours in any degree of dogmatism. If, therefore, I complain of my right honourable friend the Chancellor of the Exchequer in this matter, it is not because I am not willing to give the best consideration in my power to any proposal which the Government may make with the view of improving the constitution of this House; but although I am perfectly ready to entertain such a question, I do think it is but fair to existing institutions to say that the burden of proof is in their favour—that the presumption is in favour of that which is until it is removed by some argument which shows that that can be replaced by something better. The way in which the Chancellor of the Exchequer

proposed this great change, without condescending to
offer a word depreciatory of the present system, to point
out its faults and suggest remedies for them, leads to
the conclusion that he assumed the burden of proof
to be in the opposite direction to that which I have
indicated, and that the defenders of the Constitution
are bound to answer in the first instance the arguments of the innovators, instead of waiting until the
latter have made out their case. I, for one, deprecate
that spirit of innovation which assumes that what
exists is wrong, and introduces a proposal which distinctly calls upon us to pull down the noble work of
our forefathers before a single word is said to show
why we should assail it. The Chancellor of the Exchequer found plenty of time to deal with a great
many subjects much less important. He discussed
with the utmost sagacity and felicity the difference
between "annual value" and "gross estimated rental,"
while he was eloquent in distinctions—in which we
could not all follow him—with respect to compound
householders, tenants of flats, lodgers, and other abstruse personalities. But, although he ably entered
into all these matters, and with a detail which reminds
me more of a speech on the Budget than on Reform,
he did not find—so pinched was he for time—a
moment to say a single word why the Constitution
under which we have lived so long might not be left
to us a little longer.

Passing from that subject, I will state in a few

words to the House all that I deem it to be necessary
to address to them with respect to the Bill which the
right honourable gentleman asks leave to introduce.
This Bill proposes, in short, to increase the whole
electors of the country, whom he estimates at 900,000,
by 400,000—that is to say, nearly one-third. [An
honourable MEMBER: One-half.] Yes, one-half of
the present constituency, but only one-third of that
which will exist if the Bill passes into law. That is,
nearly one-half of the existing number, and one-third
of what the number would be. He proposes to make
in the counties 171,000 new electors, and in the
boroughs 204,000, the latter being almost altogether
derived from the single class of persons renting at
10*l.*, or under 10*l.* It will be almost entirely so, but
there may be some slight difference—144,000 are
absolutely and the rest pretty nearly so. With regard
to the county franchise, I have only one observation
to make. The proposition of the Chancellor of the
Exchequer will very much enlarge the electoral area,
enormously increase the expense of elections, and
create a great re-distribution of political power. That
may be right, or it may be wrong, but before we pass
it we should be told the reason why. Then coming
to the boroughs, the case is much more serious. The
right honourable gentleman opposed the voters in
counties as being of the middle class to the voters in
boroughs as being of the working class; and, according to the right honourable gentleman's showing, if

this Bill pass, we are to have 330,000 voters in the constituencies belonging to the working class, and 360,000 in the constituencies not working men. That is the system he proposes for our adoption. This leads us to a very grave consideration, because not only the statement of the right honourable gentleman, but the statistics laid before the House, show that the number of persons belonging to the working class already admitted to the franchise is 126,000, or about one-fifth of the whole amount of electors. That is a most grave and momentous fact. Look what it proves. It proves in the first place that the Government were entirely mistaken as regards the main ground on which they introduced the present measure. The main ground they put forth for bringing in the Bill—until they came to bring it in, when they thought it expedient to put forth no ground at all—was that the best of the working class were excluded from the franchise. The authority on which I make this statement is an authority which no one can dispute—it is a work on the English Government and Constitution issued by Lord Russell twice in the course of last year—once in the spring, and again in the autumn. This is a passage from the preface to the work—

" But may there not be still improvements?"
—in the Reform Bill, the noble Lord means; and this is the answer he gives—

" Each of the last four Ministries have been willing

" to add as it were a supplement to the Reform Act.
" For my part, I should be glad to see the sound
" morals and clear intelligence of the working classes
" more fully represented. They are kept out of the
" franchise, which Ministers of the Crown have re-
" peatedly asked for them, partly by the jealousy of
" the present holders of the suffrage, and partly by a
" vague fear that, by their greater numbers, they will
" swallow up all other classes. Both those obstacles
" may be removed by a judicious modification of the
" proposed suffrage."

That proves most clearly that, in the opinion of
Lord Russell as expressed last autumn, the best of the
working classes had not the franchise. Is that true?
Take the right honourable gentleman's own statistics
in your hands, and compare them with that preface.
Can you reconcile them? No, for they are absolutely
irreconcilable. It is quite clear that Earl Russell
wrote under a delusion, which was shared in by every
gentleman who used the argument, and that, I believe,
comprehended almost every gentleman on the Treasury
Bench. He was under the delusion, that we all more
or less shared in and believe, that the working classes
were excluded from the franchise, and that there was
a sharp line drawn at the 10l. franchise, above which
the working men could not penetrate. That being
the whole proposition which the noble lord put forward with respect to Reform, and that being proved
to be founded upon a mistake, I want to know upon

what principle it is that the Government, having
received the statistics which my noble friend the
member for Haddingtonshire (Lord Elcho) advised
them to obtain, showing that these people, for the
sake of whom they asked for a Reform Bill, were
already represented—I want to know why they now
go on at all with a bill in respect of the representation
of the people. Surely this was worth explaining. We
could have perfectly understood it if these statistics
had not been there ; my right honourable friend would
have told us at once that it was to enfranchise the
working men ; but these facts being as they are, my
right honourable friend says absolutely nothing, but
assumes that this House is going to entertain a proposition without knowing in the least what his adhe-
sion to it in his own mind is based upon, or what
reason there is for asking the House to accede to it.
These statistics prove a little more. They prove a
thing for saying which I have been greatly reproved
—that the franchise was, in fact, in the power to a
great extent of the working classes. I have been
reviled in the best and in the worst of English for
the statement, and nobody has taken me to task
more severely than the noble lord whose Preface I
have read, because he has introduced a fresh series of
paragraphs into his Preface to the last edition merely
for the purpose of castigating me for saying anything
so unkind and so untrue as that the franchise was in
their power. All I can say is, if it is not in their

power, how did they get there? These statistics
prove something more still, and what is also very
well worth the notice of the Government. It is this:
I do not apprehend we have any statistics to show us
when it was that this great increase in the constituencies took place, but I think no one who knows
the history of this country can doubt that it is owing
to the great expansion of everything during the last
twenty or thirty years. We know the causes at work
which produced the expansion, but are they permanent or are they transient? The first cause was
undoubtedly the discovery of gold in California and
Australia, and the consequent depreciation of the
precious metals gave an apparent increase of prices
both in wages and in commodities. This led to
higher rents and to higher wages—though I do not
wish to embarrass the subject by going into figures.
Another cause which kept up the rate of wages was
the great emigration which took place, and is still
taking place, from Ireland. Another cause was the
vast extension in our trade and commerce, making
labour every day more and more in demand. Therefore, I am not wrong, I think, in considering that
these causes which have existed hitherto have their
efficacy by no means spent, and what we have a right
to look at is, that the process of spontaneous enfranchisement that has been going on since the passing of
the Reform Bill will go on hereafter, and probably
with redoubled vigour. We have to build upon an

admission—I cannot extract many principles from
the Chancellor of the Exchequer's speech, but it is
impossible to manipulate figures and statements
without implying something—and one thing that
he laid down was that he did not wish to see the
working classes in a majority in the constituencies in
this country; at least, he said he did not much care
himself, but for the sake of weaker brethren he would
not like to see that. And, therefore, he rejected—
with a bitter pang, no doubt—the 6l. franchise, and
took the 7l., because the 6l. would have given 428,000,
which would have been a clear majority of 362,000,
whereas the 7l. franchise gives 330,000, which leaves
a very small majority the other way. But it must be
remembered that we are not speaking for a year or
two, but for the future, and I would ask the House
what are the prospects of the constituencies—what
are the chances that the principle which the Chancellor of the Exchequer could not screw his nerves up
to face, would remain inviolate? Is it not certain that
in a few years from this the working men will be in a
majority? Is it not certain that causes are at work
which will have a tendency to multiply the franchise
—that the 6l. houses will become the 7l. ones, and
the 9l. houses will expand to 10l.? There is no
doubt an immense power of expansion; and therefore, without straining anything at all, it is certain
that sooner or later we shall see the working classes
in a majority in the constituencies. Look at what

that implies. I shall speak very frankly on this subject, for having lost my character by saying that the
working man could get the franchise for himself, which
has been proved to be true, and for saying which he
and his friends will not hate me one bit the less, I
shall say exactly what I think. Let any gentleman
consider—I have had such unhappy experiences, and
many of us have—let any gentleman consider the
constituencies he has had the honour to be concerned
with. If you want venality, if you want ignorance,
if you want drunkenness, and facility for being inti-
midated; or if, on the other hand, you want impulsive, unreflecting, and violent people, where do you
look for them in the constituencies? Do you go to
the top or to the bottom? It is ridiculous for us
to allege, that since the Reform Bill the sins of the
constituencies or the voters are mainly comprised
between 20*l.* and 10*l.* But, then, it has been said,
the 10*l.* shopkeepers, and lodging-house keepers,
and beer-house keepers, are an indifferent class of
people; but get to the artisan, and there you will
see the difference. It is the sort of theory the
ancients had about the north wind. The ancients
observed that as they went farther to the north the
wind got colder. Colder and colder it got the farther
they went, just as the constituencies get worse and
worse the nearer you approach 10*l.* They reasoned
in this way: If it is so cold when you are in front of
the north wind, how very warm it would be if you

could only get behind it! And, therefore, they imagined for themselves a blessed land we have all read
of, where the people called the Hyperboreans were
always perfectly warm, happy, and virtuous, because
they had got to the other side of the north wind. It
is the same view that my right honourable friend
takes with respect to the 10*l.* franchise—if you go a
little lower, you get into the virtuous stratum. We
know what those persons are who live in small houses
—we have had experience of them under the name
of "freemen"—and no better law, I think, could
have been passed than that which disfranchised
them altogether. The Government are proposing to
enfranchise one class of men who have been disfranchised heretofore. This class, dying out under
one name, the Government propose to bring back
under another. That being so, I ask the House to
consider what good we are to get for the country at
large by this reduction of the franchise? The effect
will manifestly be to add a large number of persons
to our constituencies of the class from which, if
there is to be anything wrong going on, we may
naturally expect to find it. It will increase the
expenses of candidates—it will enormously increase
the expenses of management of elections, even supposing that everything is conducted in a legitimate
and fair manner—and it will very much increase the
expenses of electioneering altogether. If experience
proves that corruption varies inversely as the franchise,

you must look for more bribery and corruption than you have hitherto had.   This will be the first and instantaneous result.   Then, there is another which I wish to point out to honourable gentlemen on this side of the House—their own experience will bear me out if they would frankly admit it—and that is, that by a singular retribution of Providence the main mischief will fall on the promoters of this Bill.   A great many of these new electors are addicted to Conservative opinions ; I do believe the franchise of the Government, if carried, will displace a number of most excellent gentlemen on this side, and replace them with an equal number of gentlemen from the other side of the House.   But all this is merely the first stage. The first stage, I have no doubt, will be an increase of corruption, intimidation, and disorder, of all the evils that happen usually in elections.   But what will be the second ?   The second will be that the working men of England, finding themselves in a full majority of the whole constituency, will awake to a full sense of their power.   They will say, " We can do better for " ourselves.   Don't let us any longer be cajoled at " elections.   Let us set up shop for ourselves.   We " have objects to serve as well as our neighbours, and " let us unite to carry those objects.   We have ma- " chinery ; we have our trades unions ; we have our " leaders all ready.   We have the power of combina- " tion, as we have shown over and over again ; and " when we have a prize to fight for we will bring it to

" bear, with tenfold more force than ever before."
Well, when that is the case—when you have a Parliament appointed, as it will be, by such constituencies
so deteriorated—with a pressure of that kind brought
to bear, what is it you expect Parliament to stop at?
Where is the line that can be drawn? The right
honourable gentleman has said to us, that he does not
pledge Government to any re-distribution of seats;
but if the Government should bring it forward he
thinks this Parliament might be kept alive in order to
effect that re-distribution. I am very much obliged to
my right honourable friend; but, for my part, I think
Parliamentary life would not be worth preserving on
those terms. Look at the position Parliament will
occupy. As long as we have not passed this Bill, we
are masters of the situation. Let us pass the Bill, and
in what position are we? That of the Gibeonites—
hewers of wood and drawers of water, rescued for a
moment from the slaughter that fell on the other
Canaanites in order that we may prepare the Bill for
re-distribution, with a threat hanging over our heads
that if we do not do the work we shall be sent about
our business and make way for another Parliament.

Thus much for the two main features of the Bill.
But there is another feature in the Bill—that it is
only a Franchise Bill, and does not deal with the redistribution of seats at all. That was the advice given
to the Government by the honourable member for
Birmingham in his speech at Rochdale, and they

have followed his advice. I do not make it matter of cavil against them that they did so. It is lawful to be taught by an enemy; how much more by a friend! But the honourable member for Birmingham was not always of this opinion. I will read a passage from a speech of his which, I think, will convey a rather different impression—

"Repudiate without mercy any Bill of any Govern-
"ment, whatever its franchise, whatever its seeming
"concession, may be, if it does not distribute the
"seats which are obtained by the extinction of small
"boroughs mainly among the great cities and towns
"of the kingdom."

MR. BRIGHT: What are you reading from?

MR. LOWE: I will tell the honourable member, —but he has made so many speeches that it is not always easy to distinguish which,—I am quoting from the speech delivered by him in 1859 at Bradford. There is a little bit more yet. He says—

"The question of distribution is the very soul of
"the question, and unless you get that you will be
"deceived, and when the Bill is passed you may
"possibly have to lament that you are not in the posi-
"tion in which you would wish to find yourself."

I read this not for the purpose of getting a laugh at the honourable member for Birmingham, though I have no particular objection to that: I read it in order to point out to the House the working of the honourable gentleman's mind. I have not the least doubt that the honourable member for Birmingham, notwithstanding the apparent inconsistency of his speeches at Rochdale and Bradford, was perfectly consistent all the while. I believe he always had distinctly in view the re-distribution of seats. He has certain objects to obtain—which are not my objects, nor are they, I believe, the objects of many members of the House—and having those objects, the honourable gentleman felt, I think very justly, upon consideration, that the way to get a re-distribution of seats—at least such a re-distribution as he wants—is not to seek for it in the first instance. The present constituencies do not furnish a sufficiently powerful instrument for the purpose. He wanted an instrument to pulverize the representation, and therefore, like a good workman, he says, "Let us make the " tools first, and then we shall speedily construct the " machine." The tools for the construction of that machine are the House to be created by the Bill of the Government, brought in at his own instance, excluding the consideration of the re-distribution of seats until the Franchise Bill shall be carried, and an Assembly much more democratic in its nature than the present can be brought together. That is what I have to say with regard to the Bill of the Government. We shall have an opportunity of considering it on the second reading, but I earnestly hope that honourable gentlemen will weigh what I have said.

And remember this, that there is another principle

assumed throughout the speech of the Chancellor of
Exchequer, which is this—that you cannot possibly
make constituencies too large so long as you do not
put flagrantly improper people into them. That is, I
believe, a mistake. It is quite possible to make constituencies so large as to deter from sitting in this
House men of moderate opinions and moderate means
who would be very valuable members. It is easy to
conceive that constituencies may be so large as to
divide the representation between millionaires, to
whom any expense is of no moment, and demagogues,
who compensate for want of money by pandering to
popular passions. The House must remember that
members of Parliament have thrown on them another
duty than that of merely representing the people. It
has been ever since the Revolution of 1688, and, if we
do not destroy the conditions under which the arrangement subsists, it will continue to be the happy lot of
this country, that the leading offices of the executive
Government have only approached it through the
vestibule of the House of Commons. If you form
your House solely with a view to numbers, solely
with a view to popular representation, whatever other
good you obtain you will destroy the element out of
which your statesmen must be made. You will lower
the position of the executive Government, and render
it difficult, if not impossible, to carry on that happy
union between the two powers which now exists.
The Reform Bill of 1832 has certainly invigorated our

legislation ; but it may be a question whether it has been equally efficient in invigorating our executive Government.

And here, if I have not already trespassed too much on the indulgence of the House, I would just pause to inquire what reasons can possibly be alleged —the Government have given us none—for bringing in this Bill at all. Is it that it is demanded out of doors ? The working classes have gone very wisely, as I myself would go, ten miles to hear the honourable member for Birmingham ; but have they demanded this Bill ? Has there been any energy in the demand for such a franchise as this? There have been meetings at St. Martin's Hall and elsewhere, but the resolutions have always been for universal suffrage. ["No, no!"] Almost uniformly they have spoken very disrespect-fully of the honourable member for Leeds and his proposition. Have any petitions been presented for this Bill ? The last account I heard of the petitions was that four had been presented; how many more are there ? Those who met in St. Martin's Hall have spoken out. Mr. Odgers moved the first resolu-tion, but what he said he wanted was an Act of Parlia-ment to keep up wages. There was another man, a mason, I think, who soared to a higher degree of patriotism, and asked, " Why don't you pass an Act of " Parliament to make Ireland happy at once ?" I therefore conclude that there is no very overwhelming pressure for Reform from that quarter yet. Is it from

the constituencies the pressure comes? Why, I have
read a passage from Lord Russell's letter in which he
says that it is on account of the selfishness of the constituencies that the working men are kept out. That
is, in other words, the constituencies are not favourable
to Reform. Well, is it from the members of this
House? There, again, I call the same witness. The
noble Earl said to a deputation which went to him
with very extreme views on the subject of Reform, "I
"agree with you in most of what you have said; but I
"anticipate the greatest difficulty from the House of
"Commons." Lastly—and owing to the delicacy of the
question I would not put it, only the public interests
require that I should do so—is it from the Cabinet?
There, again, I call on Lord Russell, because the
honourable gentleman the member for Birmingham
asserted at a meeting that on the occasion of receiving
a deputation, or on some other occasion, he found the
noble Lord as ardent as possible for Reform, but that
he told him he had immense difficulties to deal with
in his Cabinet.

MR. BRIGHT: I do not know whether the right
honourable gentleman was at that meeting; but I
say that there is not a word of truth in the statement. Lord Russell has never said one word to me
that would in any way inform me what the opinion
of any member of his Cabinet was. I have no
recollection of having said anything such as the
right honourable gentleman alleges. If he is quoting

anything that he has read, it is something which
I never said—something which was incorrectly reported.

Mr. Lowe: I have no wish to persevere in attributing anything to the honourable gentleman which
he denies having said. What I have quoted I read
in *The Star*, though, of course, I am quoting from
memory. I take in *The Star* when I want any information about the honourable member. Well, now
let us come to reason on the thing. It is said that it
is in deference to public opinion this Bill is brought
in. It is not because the working man is excluded.
I have shown that. But the Chancellor of the Exchequer says that honourable gentlemen on both
sides have entered this House committed to Reform.
Now, this is a question of high morality, and I wish
honourable gentlemen to turn this matter seriously
in their minds. I apprehend that any gentleman who
enters this House does not enter it as the member for
any particular borough or county, but as a representative of the whole country ; and he enters it bound by
an obligation which no promise he has given can add
to, or take away from, one jot or tittle. That obligation is, that to the best of his ability he will honestly
do his duty to the country. Well, then, if a gentleman finds himself hampered by pledges which touch
his honour, there is always a course open to him to
take. If he has got into a situation incompatible
with honour, he should get out of it. If he remain

in it, he will be in that position described by one of
our greatest poets—

> " His honour in rooted dishonour stood,
>   And faith unfaithful made him falsely true."

I hope, therefore, whatever may be the fate of this
question, we shall not hear that honourable gentlemen
are pledged to act contrary to their consciences, and
to do what they believe will be injurious to their
country.

I have now very little more to add in respect of
the reasons for introducing this measure. I find
nothing so difficult as to get a Reformer to assign his
reasons. The plan is to assume that there are reasons. Bring in the Bill, *solvitur ambulando*, by
walking into the subject. In the arguments put
forward on this subject we very seldom hear a gentleman take it up and argue it from the beginning, so
as to show us why we should have reform at all. I do
not now say we should not have it ; but I say that you
should not argue the Reform question as if the franchise were a boon which you had at your disposal,
and of which you should make an equal distribution.
You should not deal with it as if it were the Banda
and Kirwee prize money which you were going to
distribute. Is it a consideration of that kind which
should form part of the political system of a great
Empire ? In fact, we have *à priori* grounds of all
kinds alleged. But the franchise is not to be given

on an *à priori* principle of justice. This is not a
question to be decided *à priori*, or on what a gentleman can evolve from the depths of his inner consciousness. It is a question of practical experience of
the working of our laws—one as to the best machinery
we can have for the work we have to do. I can well
understand how such notions get root among the
people. When the common people are told that
there is anything to be got, they think that, as in the
administration of justice, there should be equality
to all. They think the Government ought to distribute everything equally, as if something was to be
divided between co-partners. But that is an entire
misunderstanding of the real business of a Government. Government does not deal with justice—it
deals with expediency. The object is to construct the
best machinery for the purpose to which it is to
be applied. We may violate any law of symmetry,
equality, or distributive justice in providing the
proper machinery to enable us to do what is required
of us. That being so, I will now state what I think
the Government really ought to have done, and which
it has not done. As this Bill, though it works on the
constituencies, really is a Bill to alter the constitution
of the House, and to redistribute power in the House,
I say it is the bounden duty of the Government to
begin their inquiries by a minute examination of the
state of this House—to see wherein it has succeeded
and wherein it has failed. When that is done, let

them still further improve what they find good, if
they can do so, and remedy what they find to
have failed. It is the duty of the Government,
like any other physicians, to study the case with
which they have to deal. If they do otherwise, they
are acting like a physician who spends his time in
mixing drugs and sharpening lancets, and never
takes the trouble to see what is the matter with his
patient. As the Government do not appear to have
conducted such an examination as I have suggested,
perhaps we may with advantage do a little in this
way for ourselves. I have the most unfeigned respect
and veneration for this House, and therefore I should
not wish to see its constitution altered without good
grounds; but let us try to do what is the most difficult of all things—let us endeavour to acquire self-
knowledge ; let us try "to see ourselves as others see
" us." This House has been called the "mirror of
" the nation," as if the nation had nothing to do but
look at this House in order to see itself as in a look-
ing-glass. Now, I want the House to look at itself
in this mirror. I think, then, we may say, without
self-praise, that this House holds—not only in England, but throughout the whole world—a position far
above that ever held by any other deliberative Assembly that ever existed. It is more respected all
over the world, its debates are more read, and they
exercise more influence on mankind than those of
assemblies infinitely more popular. Ought we not to

be proud, then, of the position which this House
occupies in the body politic of nations? Well, I
think I may go further, and say that the functions
which it has principally to discharge—those of finance
—it has discharged with greater success than any
other deliberative assembly. Of course it is not perfect, nothing human is. I dare say there are people
who think that the votes for the army and navy are
outdoor relief for the aristocracy, that the Church is
in the same category, and so forth; but the majority
of the people of this country are satisfied that the
finances are managed by the House in a manner
creditable both to the House and the nation. If I go
further, it must be said of this House that it never
has been deaf to any appeal for the protection of the
humbler classes. I know there is a clamour that the
poor man is not represented in this House. But can
any one say that the interests of the poor are neglected here? Look to the debates we have had on
the cases of poor women who have been removed in
steamers from this country to Ireland. In this House
immediate attention is given to everything affecting
the poor. It is impossible to find a remedy always,
but such cases always receive attention. I will not
say what this House has done in legislation; I said
it last year, and I will not repeat it. But I think I
may say this House is a very orderly assembly—one
of the most orderly of deliberate assemblies. When
we go to other places—and, indeed, we need not go

farther than a place not a hundred miles from us—we find that the House of Commons will bear comparison with any other assembly for the regularity of its proceedings. It is independent also. Whatever may have happened a hundred years ago, no one will say that there is any personal corruption in the House of Commons now. It is industrious, too. We labour more hours, and get through a greater amount of business than any other assembly in the world. These are great merits. I want to know, will the Bill which the Government have proposed leave all these things as it finds them? Will the constituencies in their altered character have no influence on the House? As the polypus takes its colour from the rock to which it affixes itself, so do the Members of this House take their character from the constituencies. If you lower the character of the constituencies, you lower that of the representatives, and you lower the character of this House. I do not want to say anything disagreeable, but if you want to see the result of democratic constituencies, you will find them in all the assemblies of Australia, and in all the assemblies of North America. But this House, like all human institutions, possesses imperfections, and I will point out one or two of them. In the first place, a great change has been operating since the year 1832, which no one has noticed, but which, I think, ought to have been taken into consideration. That change is this, that the House of Commons is now much nearer its

constituents and much more influenced by them than
it was before. In old days, when a man left his constituents, there was a great gulf between him and
them, but now the constituents have a second function in addition to electing their Members. They
can communicate with them by railway and by
telegraph, and sometimes it has happened that
the vote of a Member has been changed in the
course of a debate by a telegram received from
his constituents. A measure is sometimes proposed
but not fully gone into, and the local press, though
insufficiently informed on the question, takes it up
and argues upon it, and the result is that the constituents make up their mind on the subject before
they have heard the real issue to be raised, and
they force their conclusions on their representatives,
though these may be far better informed. The less
informed tribunal, therefore, acquires more influence
than it should over the superior and better informed
tribunal. These are small blots, perhaps, but they
are worth mentioning, because I want to ask whether
more democratic constituencies would be inclined
to give their Members more freedom than they have
at present? Would they be more tolerant of the
opinions of the honest and able man who does not follow the whim of the moment? Would they be more
patient, more tolerant, and more inclined to respect
real dignity and consistency of character than they
are now? Then there is another subject, and a very

serious one indeed, which I have already touched upon—that is, the relations subsisting between this House and the executive Government. Now this House and the executive Government working together form a most invaluable institution. The House derives support from having a Government to lead it, dignity from its power of access to the very fountains of all political knowledge, and authority and information from being able to exercise the privilege of interrogating the Ministers of the Crown—a privilege of which it has largely availed itself this evening. On the other hand, the Ministers of the Crown derive strength, and many advantages, from being placed in immediate contact with the Legislature. They are not placed in a position like that of the Secretary of Finance in America, who is obliged to get a private member to propose his financial measures. Here all the departments of the Government are represented— its members sit in this House, and have in debate the support and assistance of their friends and colleagues when the policy of the Government is attacked. I hold, therefore, that they gain infinitely by contact with each other, and that anything which would tend to sever the connection between them must be dangerous and most mischievous. It is painful to observe that the first Reform Bill, however successful it may have been in legislation, has not been equally successful in this matter. Since I have had the honour of sitting here, it has been painful to observe the increas-

ing weakness of the executive Government in this
House. Formerly, if a gentleman moved for papers
which, in the opinion of the Government, ought not to
be produced, or which it would be unwise to put the
country to the expense of printing, the Ministers resisted the motion, and inconvenience or expense was
saved to the public. But who resists such motions
now? Formerly, if a committee were asked for, to inquire into a subject which had been already threshed
out and examined into, or one which it was not
proper to investigate, the Minister of the department
to which it related could get up in his place and say,
" I cannot grant such a committee." What Minister
can say so now? Our ancestors, when they had once
settled in their own minds that a thing was right,
acted according to their convictions. Now, however,
if a question is important and difficult, it is delegated
to a committee; if not to a committee, to a commis-
sion, or it is delegated to some local authority, or it is
made an open question. The whole machinery, in
fact, has fallen a great deal too much into the hands
of this House, and the effect necessarily must be, if
the process goes on, to injure the influence and standing of this House; because, if the House should
appoint a committee to transact the business of every
public office behind the Minister, it would incur an
immense amount of responsibility and blame which is
now laid upon the shoulders of the executive Government, and which the Government on its dissolution

carries away with it as the scapegoat carried on its
head the sins of the whole congregation. All these
things are matters of very serious importance. You
are aware that the wise men who founded the Constitution of America knew that, with its democratic
foundation, it would be absolutely impossible to have
the English system, so they established a system
under which the executive Government and the Legislature should exist for a different period of years,
and should be elected by different authorities, in order
that they might have no point of contact with each
other. The feebleness which that quality imparted to
the Executive and the Legislature in America may be
seen in the discord which has broken out between the
head of the Executive and the Legislature. So long
as we retain our present constitution, such a state of
things could not exist for a moment in this country.
And, therefore, it seems to me quite evident, that if
this House means to maintain the great power and influence which it exercises over the executive Government, it must beware of putting itself on too democratic
a foundation. In proportion as it does so it will lose
the power of working the existing system, until at last
it will be driven, as the Australian and other colonies
will ultimately be driven, to appoint the Executive for
a number of years certain, whether the Executive be,
or whether it be not, in harmony with the Legislature
of the time. Now, I ask the House again whether,
with America and Australia before us, and with proof

that it is the democratic state of their society and institutions which mainly renders a system like ours
unworkable in those countries, it is wise in us to push
forward in a direction which, though it may make this
House more popular, will deprive it of the noblest
property it possesses, that of working in accordance
with the executive Government? Then, again, elections are day by day becoming more expensive—I
refer, of course, to legitimate expenses. It is not
difficult to account for this. A torrent of wealth is
flowing into the country, and persons naturally seek a
seat in this House—some for political purposes, and
some for purposes non-political. There are, for instance, the representatives of great companies and
great interests, and gentlemen wishing to get into
society under the stimulus of their wives and daugh-
ters. I say that this is a most serious matter, because
is is only through this House that the most important
members of the Government can enter the Government; and if you require, in addition to the immense
labour and the vicissitudes to which public life is subject, that the aspirants to office should expend more in
conciliating their electors than they receive from the
public, you will make public life impossible to the
class of men which you wish to have. I ask the Chancellor of the Exchequer how long he thinks the small
boroughs would exist after a democratic Constitution
has been brought into effect—those small boroughs on
behalf of which he made so eloquent a speech in 1859,

as the places which sent to Parliament such men as
Chatham, Pitt, Fox, Canning, and Peel? How long
does he think those boroughs would survive the measure which he has brought in without a word of
explanation on this important branch of the subject?
And will the right honourable gentleman tell us how,
when these boroughs are thrown away, he proposes to
supply their place? For, unless this House is willing,
like the Congress of America, to put an end altogether
to its connection with the executive Government, it is
necessary either that something of the kind should be
kept up, or other means devised for bringing about the
same result. It is better that the truth should be
told at once than that we should go on encouraging
people in the belief that the Government which we
now happily carry on can be carried on under conditions inimical to its existence.

Then there is the question of the "Private Busi-
"ness" in the House of Commons:—And I must say
that I view with the greatest jealousy and alarm the
degree to which this House has become a machine for
the transaction of what is called "Private Business."
We fancy that we are investigating the schemes of
people who have raised capital for the purpose of
carrying them out, and that we are simply ascertaining
whether the public assent ought to be given to those
schemes or not. But, in reality, we are doing nothing
of the kind. We are investigating schemes got up by
people with no capital at all, in order that they may

sell the approval of this House in the Stock Exchange.
Then, Sir, there are other affairs equally unpleasant,
such as Government subsidies and contracts. Now, I
cannot express how much I wish that an end could be
put to this state of things ; but do you think that by
lowering materially the franchise below the present
£10 you will redress any of these evils? Is it the
result of our experience, looking at America, and at the
democratic institutions there, whatever merits they
may have, that the people are jealous of the moral
character of their representatives? Did you ever
hear of a man who was ostracized from public life in
America in consequence of his having committed a
murder, a forgery, a perjury, or anything of that kind?
Things which would not be tolerated for an instant in
England are passed by without notice in America.
For, however impetuous and impatient democratic
constituencies may be of the acts of their members
in matters where their prejudices are affected, they
are singularly loose in their requirements in other
respects.

I think, then, that I have shown that such a Bill as
the Government intends to bring in, while it would
not in any degree alleviate any of the faults which I
have taken the liberty, with all respect, to point out
in the constitution of this House, would aggravate
every one of them, and there is not a single merit
described in this imperfect sketch which it would not
injuriously affect. Now, I want the Chancellor of

the Exchequer to show us how this measure would work in regard to this House. My sketch is imperfect, and possibly may be entirely erroneous, but let the Government make their sketch or theory upon the subject. Let them tell us what are the faults in the House of Commons, and how the present measure will remedy those faults; but let them not fling the measure on the table, and say that we must adopt it, without hearing one single reason in favour of, or against, a state of things which has existed so long and so happily. It has been said, indeed, that precisely the same arguments have been used now as were used in 1832; but you must remember that to make a good argument two things are requisite— first, that the principle itself be sound, and secondly, that it corresponds to the fact which it assumes. Now, the arguments against Reform, in 1832, were excellent, only they did not correspond to the facts of the case. The question which honourable gentlemen beg in representing the two cases as parallel is—Are the facts of the case now, the same as they were in 1832? Well, Sir, that is a question I am not going to enter into; but I may just point out this— that in 1832, the controversy was perfectly defined. The question was—Did the system then existing, work well or not? One side maintained that it did work well, the other contended that it did not; and the country decided very rightly, as I, for one, think, that it did not. But that is not the controversy now.

It is now admitted that the system does work well ;
and the controversy now is, ought we not still to
alter it ? Take, for instance, a very clever letter,
signed " H.," which appeared in *The Times* of yes-
terday. In reply to the question what good a Reform
Bill could be expected to accomplish, the writer
said—

" I am quite willing, for the sake of this argument,
" to answer ' none.' Nevertheless, I reply, even if
" that be so, the passing of a Reform Bill is a posi-
" tive advantage,"
—simply, as I suppose, because gentlemen are, as
they call themselves, " committed." That is, for the
sake of preserving our consistency, we are to do that
which we know to be injurious to the best interests
of the country. You must also make this distinction
between the present time and 1832. The grievances
that were complained of in 1832, were practical
grievances. Do not believe for a moment that the
House of Commons was reformed simply on account
of the anomalies of the system. The House of Commons was reformed because the public mind was
revolted by things which they thought bad in the
legislation and government of the country, and seized
upon those anomalies as the weapons to abate the
nuisance. That, being a practical grievance, has been
redressed, and led for a certain time to a settlement
of the question. But, Sir, nobody ever settles a question by remedying a mere theoretical grievance, and

H

that is just the grievance we have now to deal with.
My right honourable friend the Chancellor of the
Exchequer, told us in his speech, as one great in-
ducement to pass his Bill, that we should find in
it a complete settlement of the question, and that
he hoped that impracticable persons—I do not know
whether I was one to whom he referred—if for no
other reason, would be induced to give their assent
to the Bill, because it would be a settlement of the
question. Settlement? What significance does the
right honourable gentleman attach to that word?
He stated that you are to go on with this Bill for
twelve nights in this Session, and, if you cannot
pass it in twelve nights, it is to be left to the
charities of private members, and those charities are,
we know, very cold. Thus, probably, the measure
might go over this year, and begin over again next
year, and when we have disposed of it, we are to
be refreshed by a Franchise Bill for Scotland, and
a Franchise Bill for Ireland, about which we were
told that the information was, rather than not, in a
state of preparation. Then, when we have done with
the three Franchise Bills, three Re-distribution Bills
are to follow ; and even then we shall not be out of
the wood, because there is to be also a Boundaries
Bill, one of the most difficult and irritating subjects
which can be imagined—and, after that, we are to
come to a Registration Bill, which is also a matter of
great difficulty. We have now reckoned up eight

measures, and there is one more yet, enough to make
any man shudder to think of, and that is an anti-
corruption Bill. So that the prospect of a settlement,
which the right honourable gentleman holds out, is,
that we are to begin *de novo* with the whole of our
electoral system, and to go through the whole of it
in measures which, according to his own enumera-
tion, amount at least to nine ; and that he holds out
as a settlement; so that, if we will pass this Bill, we
may possibly, if we behave well, employ ourselves in
going through this amount of work. That, however,
is not my idea of a settlement, and I am quite sure
that, in addition to that, there are unsettling causes
which the right honourable gentleman did not tell us
of. Supposing the Bills are passed—as they will be
passed, if at all—in mere deference to numbers, at
the expense of property and intelligence, in deference
to a love of symmetry and equality—at least, that is
the name under which the democratic passion of envy
generally disguises itself, and which will only be
satisfied by symmetry and equality. I feel convinced that, when you have given all the right
honourable gentleman asks, you will still leave plenty
of inequalities, enough to stir up this passion anew.
The grievance being theoretical and not practical,
will survive as long as practice does not conform
to theory; and practice will never conform to theory
until you have got to universal suffrage and equal
electoral districts. I say, therefore, that there is

no element of finality in this measure, and though,
as I have before said, I am perfectly willing to
consider anything that may be brought forward, I
crave leave to say, that I shall consider the guidance
of my own vote and conduct with reference to its
influence on the good or bad working of the House of
Commons, and not with reference to any theories
about the ideal of good government, which, according
to one great thinker, consists in everybody having
a share in it—just, as I suppose, his ideal of a joint-
stock company is one in which everybody is a
director.

Well, Sir, the right honourable gentleman, who
had not time to give us a reason for introducing
the Bill, found time to give us a quotation; and it
was a quotation of a very curious kind, because, not
finding in his large classical *repertoire* any quotation
that would exactly describe the state of perfect bliss
to which his Bill would introduce us, he was induced
to take the exact contrary, and make a quotation
to show us what his Bill was not.

> "Scandit fatalis machina muros,
> Fœta armis,"

he exclaimed, " and that," he added, " is not my
Bill." Well, that was not a very apt quotation; but
there was a curious felicity about it which he little
dreamt of. The House remembers, that among other
proofs of the degree in which public opinion is

enlisted in the cause of Reform is this—that this
is now the fifth Reform Bill that has been brought
in since 1851. Now, just attend to the sequel of the
passage quoted by the right honourable gentleman.
I am no believer in *sortes Virgilianæ*, and the House
will see why, in a moment—

> " O Divum domus Ilium, et inclyta bello
> Mœnia Dardanidûm ! Quater ipso in limina portæ
> Substitit, atque utero sonitum quater arma dedêre."

But that is not all—

> " Instamus tamen immemores, cæcique furore,
> Et monstrum infelix sacratâ sistimus arce."

Well, I abominate the presage contained in the last
two lines ; but I mix my confidence with fear. The
intentions and actions of the new Parliament are as
yet hidden by the veil of the future. It may be that
we are destined to avoid this enormous danger with
which we are confronted, and not, to use the language of my right honourable friend, be fated to
compound with danger and misfortune. But, Sir, it
may be otherwise ; and all I can say is, that if
my right honourable friend does succeed in carrying
this measure through Parliament, when the passions
and interests of the day are gone by, I do not envy
him his retrospect. I covet not a single leaf of
the laurels that may encircle his brow. I do not
envy him his triumph. His be the glory of carrying
it ; mine of having, to the utmost of my poor ability,
resisted it.

SPEECH ON THE REPRESENTATION OF THE PEOPLE BILL.

SECOND READING.   *26th April,* 1866.

Sir, as we are now on the second reading of the
Bill for reducing the electoral franchise, it is not
inopportune to ask, what is the principle of the
Bill? Our information on that subject at the present moment is very meagre. We have heard from
my right honourable friend the President of the
Board of Trade, that the principle of the Bill is to
reduce the franchise; and we have learnt from the
Solicitor-General for Scotland, as I understood him,
that the principle of the Bill is to fill up two
blanks with figures—which the Government propose
to fill up with "seven" and "fourteen" respectively,
but which we may fill up with any numbers we
think proper. These are the rather faded and
colourless views which have been imparted to us on
this important subject. I submit that they are no
answer to the question at all; because the principle

of a Bill does not mean the scope and tenor of a
Bill. It does not mean what the Bill professes to do.
but it means the grounds and reasons on which it is
based; and on that subject, so far as I am aware, the
Government are entirely silent. I can only imagine
two grounds on which this Bill for lowering the
elective franchise can be proposed to the House.
The first of these grounds is, that the franchise is a
thing which ought to be given for its own sake ; the
second is, that it is a means for obtaining some ulterior
object. Which of these two is the principle of this
Bill? The first principle has, at any rate, the merit
of extreme simplicity. Those who possess it are very
little troubled either with proof or investigation.
According to that theory, all they have to do is to
find a person fitted to have the elective franchise—
and they are not very particular or exacting in proof
of fitness, nor very strict in the presumptions they
apply to it—and having found that person, the giving
of the franchise to him follows as a matter of immediate and cogent necessity. According to this view,
this is not a question of politics at all, but of morality
—of right and wrong. It is a "debt," to use the word
of the Chancellor of the Exchequer; and when you
find a man presumably fit for the franchise, according
to this view, you are as much bound to give it to him as
you are to pay your ordinary debts. To deliberate or
hesitate about it is an act of injustice, just as it is to
deliberate or hesitate about paying your ordinary

debts. All who are not admitted to the franchise become creditors of the State, and every hour we withhold it from them is wrong accumulated upon wrong—a denial of justice, a disgrace and opprobrium to those who withhold it. Now that is one view that may be taken. It is very important to know whether that be the view on which this Bill is brought forward, because it is a view which, whatever other merits it has, entirely eludes anything like reason or argument. It either flies so high or sinks so low that it is impossible to deal with it by argument. Those who propound it may be great philosophers—they may be inspired apostles of a new Religion of Humanity; but so far as they lay down this doctrine they are not politicians, nor do they use arguments within the range of the science or art of politics. They may, on the other hand, be victims of the most puerile fallacy. They may have mistaken the means for the end, and inferred, because we all believe, from our long experience of it, that the elective franchise is a good thing for the purpose of obtaining the end of good government, therefore it is necessarily a good thing in itself. They have this great advantage, in common with all enthusiasts and all persons believing in immediate intuition, over those who are not so fortunate, that they emancipate themselves from the necessity of looking at consequences. They are free from those complicated, embarrassing, and troublesome considerations of the collateral and future effects of measures, which perplex ordinary mortals. They avert their minds altogether from these things, and fall back on the principle that the thing is right in itself, and they disembarrass it of all consequences. That is one view that may be taken of the principle of this Bill. The second is a much humbler but a much sounder doctrine, and that is that the franchise, like every other political expedient, is a means to an end, the end being the preservation of order in the country, the keeping a just balance of classes, and the preventing any predominance or tyranny of one class over another. Now, Sir, this principle, we have been told, is not one of the principles of the British Constitution, and I will, therefore, with the permission of the House, read a few words from the preamble of a statute passed in 1429, the eighth year of Henry VI., and the first statute, as far as I am aware, that contains any declaration with regard to the electoral franchise. The words are these :

" Whereas the elections of knights of shires have " now of late been made by too great and excessive " number of people, either of small substance or of " no value, whereof every one of them pretended to " have a voice equivalent as to making such elections " with the most worthy knights and squires dwelling " within the same county."

And then follow words enacting that no man shall have a vote in the election of knights of the shire, unless he have a freehold amounting to 40s. per

annum in value. Now, look at the principles which
this preamble contains. In the first place, it recites
that too great a number of persons have taken part
in the elections, and it thus clearly contemplates the
very evil with which we are so much threatened now
in many directions — namely, the too great size of
electoral districts, the augmentation of constituencies
to a degree that makes them unmanageable. In the
next place, it clearly implies that a class may be
swamped by another class, poorer, less important, and
less entitled to weight in the country, because it
recites that most worthy knights and esquires are
overbalanced by persons of small substance, who have
voices equivalent to theirs; and in the next place it
establishes the principle that there ought to be a
certain fitness in a man before he is allowed to vote
for members of Parliament. Now those three principles are pretty well what is embodied in the doctrine
that the franchise is a means to an end, and that
doctrine, as I take it, is, that the franchise, though it
ought not necessarily to be given to every one fit
for it, should never be given to any one who is unfit.
It implies in the second place, that in giving votes
you should have regard not merely to the fitness
of the person, but to the influence which that person
or class of persons will exercise over the general well-
being of the State; and in the third place, it seems
to me clearly to imply that we ought to be careful so
to deal with the franchise that no one class may

swamp or overpower another or the other classes. I
therefore think that that ancient authority very clearly
lays down this second principle, which has at any rate
this advantage, that though we may differ as to the
quantity of the franchise, some wishing for more and
some for less, we have a common ground of argument. If the principle of expediency is conceded, we
may succeed in convincing each other of our errors, or
may come to some sort of compromise, whereas with
persons who hold the first principle there is no common ground whatever, and it is therefore of no use
attempting to reason with them, because all reasoning
must proceed on something admitted on both sides, if
conviction is to be obtained. A man who holds the
theory I do about politics, namely, that everything is
to be referred to the safety and good government of
the country, has no common point of departure with
the man who maintains, like the honourable gentleman,
the Under-Secretary of the Foreign Office, that it is
better we should be governed by large representative
bodies and governed badly, than governed by small
representative bodies and governed well. And now,
Sir, I ask, which of these two is the principle of this
Bill? and, in order to ascertain that, I should wish to
ascertain what the Bill will do, and what will be the
number of persons who will be enfranchised under it.
If I know that, and if I know also the manner in
which those numbers will be distributed, I have
then *data* in my own mind from which I can argue

to my own satisfaction as to what is the ground of this Bill, and what Her Majesty's Government intend by it. But, Sir, I am met here by an immense difficulty, and a difficulty entirely created by the Government themselves; for it is impossible for me, as things stand at present, to guide the vote I am asked to give, either by reference to the number of persons who will have the franchise, or by reference to the manner in which they will be distributed. The Government has that information in its hand, but it chooses, for reasons which I will consider presently, to withhold that information from the House, and to insist upon our coming to a conclusion without it.

Now, Sir, when this Bill was first brought in, it was intended, I have no doubt—in fact, it was clearly apparent—to be merely a Bill for the extension of the franchise, and the Chancellor of the Exchequer very properly acted on a principle which I never heard of any Government deviating from before. The Chancellor of the Exchequer, in order to assist our deliberations, laid before us the statistics of what would be done by the proposed change, and whether we agree to the principle or not, nothing could be more satisfactory. But then, when certain members pressed them, the Government began to slide. They slid first by saying, as the Chancellor of the Exchequer did, that they would lay a Bill for the redistribution of seats on the table. Advancing a little farther still, they said they would not only lay a Bill on the table, but would proceed with it as soon as ever they could ; and growing bolder the farther they went, they gave us the usual formula, which now seems to apply to every act of the Government, that they were prepared to "stand or fall" by it. But now that we have got to this point the case is changed. Her Majesty's Government, when they made up their minds at any rate to bring in a Redistribution Bill and stand or fall by it, had really but one course to pursue in common fairness to the House and to themselves, and that was to withdraw the Franchise Bill, and bring in a Bill combining both measures. To downright plain common sense there was no alternative, and had the matter been resolved on at once, I have no doubt it would have been done. But it was wrung from them little by little, and self-love, and pride, and a number of other motives which I shall not stop to enumerate, induced them, while they believed themselves forced to concede a great deal, to appear to concede as little as possible, and so they clung to this shred of withholding information from us, and upon that they have made it plain that they are going to put not only their Bill, but the Administration itself in peril. Now, Sir, 1 confess that I have never read of or seen any conduct on the part of any Government so utterly irrational as this. It is quite clear, that till we know how these seats are to be distributed we do not know the number of electors that this Bill will bring into existence ; because, suppose the seats of the small

boroughs—take any you like, and there is one which
people would rather take than any other—take any
you please, and take Burnley or any such place, and
transfer the seat from one borough to the other, and
it is not merely a transfer of an amount of political
power, but you call into existence several thousands
of 7l. voters, who had no electoral existence before.
So it is right we should know what number of persons
we are going to enfranchise, it is right we should also
know what the redistribution is to be. But that is not
all. The honourable member for Birmingham said the
other night, and said with truth, that you might have
universal suffrage established by law, but giving the
redistribution to a person adverse to that, he could
contrive completely to neutralize it, and could make
matters worse—that is, as the honourable member
means, less popular—than at present. Thus we are not
only in ignorance of the number of people to be enfranchised, but utterly in ignorance of what is to be
the effect of it. We do not know in the least what the
effect will be, and yet the position of the Government
is, that we are to go on and read this measure a second
time, while they, having this information in their
possession, speaking to us, and arguing with us, with
all this knowledge in their hands, withhold it from us,
and insist that we shall vote upon this measure without it. Now it is very common and very right for
Governments, when there are matters which, on the
ground of public policy, should not be made known,

to call upon their supporters, and even on the opposition in some cases, to give them so much confidence
as to allow them to keep back information. But this
is no matter of that kind. This is a matter, as far as
I can understand, kept back through mere wantonness—a trial of power to see whether the Government
can make the House of Commons pass under the yoke
or not, to see whether they can exhibit us to the
country as persons who are content to be treated with
this degree of indignity, who, before we have any
opportunity of committing ourselves, of saying or
doing anything which would lead the Government to
suppose that we are unwilling to pass this measure,
are subjected to the indignity of having the most
important of its provisions concealed from us, and
told to vote just as if we had them before us. Look
at the language which Ministers employ in speaking
of the House of Commons. The Chancellor of the
Exchequer, speaking to an applauding audience at
Liverpool, deliberately tells them that he knows the
people with whom he has to deal ; that is, of course, that
we—I do not speak of myself or of those honourable
members who have been exposed to so much animad-
version, but the House of Commons at large—are
people better known than trusted. Look, too, at the
manner in which my right honourable friend, the
President of the Board of Trade, speaks of us. He told
us the other night that he wanted to bring the matter
before us pure and simple, to get us into a corner and

compel us to speak. Now, is that a respectful manner for a Minister of the Crown to speak of the House of Commons? If it was a question of a horse, and he wanted to try whether it was a roarer, I could understand his getting it into a corner of the stable and giving it a hard punch in the ribs, to see whether it would grunt or not, but I really did think that the Commons of England were not exactly persons to be treated in this manner. But look at the right honourable gentleman the Chancellor of the Duchy of Lancaster. He said with much unction, "Some people " say we have divided this Bill into two halves, because " we knew we could not carry the whole at once, but " that we can carry it if we can cut it in two; well, " that," he says, "is exactly why we did it." That is to say, the Chancellor of the Exchequer, and the President of the Board of Trade, want to force us, to compel us; and the Chancellor of the Duchy of Lancaster, with admirable candour, says he hopes he can take us in. He thinks we are not aware that two halves make a whole, and therefore that he can palm upon us one half and then another, the two being much larger than the whole; and he thinks we shall be willing to accept them from him, and shall not be able to see through the deceit, even when he has been so kind as elaborately to explain it. It has always been said, and more particularly by Hallam, that one of the great advantages of having the leading members of the Government in this House is, that they

owe a double allegiance—one as servants of the
Crown, and another as members of the House of
Commons; so that, while not wanting in their duty
as servants of the Crown, they have always been
anxious to maintain the dignity and privileges of this
House. Hallam was a good historian, but he was no
prophet. Had he had the happiness of witnessing
the conduct of the present Government, he would
have found that, whatever their allegiance to the
Crown, the main object of their action, upon which
they are staking their very existence, is to humiliate
and degrade the members of this House in the eyes
of their constituents. The Chancellor of the Exchequer, the leader of this House, has evidently no
confidence in us. If we have no confidence in him,
we know well enough what must happen. But, although he makes a parade of a feeling of disrespect
for us, while he seeks to place us in the most humi-
liating position, we are asked to put the most implicit
confidence in him. This is not a course that the
dignity and position of this House will permit you to
adopt, and I might paraphrase an old epigram, and
say to the right honourable gentleman—

> "Whatever the pain it may cost,
>   It is time we should each say adieu;
> For your confidence in us is lost,
>   And we've not got sufficient for two."

The position held by the right honourable gentleman
is a most remarkable one, and but few men could get

into such a position twice in their lives, yet the Chancellor of the Exchequer has had that unapproachable felicity. When he went as High Commissioner Extraordinary, under the Government of Lord Derby, to the Ionian Islands, the right honourable gentleman proposed to reform the Ionian Constitution, and one of the reforms was, that the powers of the Lord High Commissioner should be defined by an Act of the Assembly. They were very sweeping and arbitrary. But he said there must be an exception to the rule, and that exception must be of all the powers that Her Majesty by Order in Council chose to exempt from the operation of the Act. You need not wonder that the Act did not pass. But let us look a little farther. I have shown—and I do not propose to dwell upon that point, because it has been so admirably put by the noble lord the member for King's Lynn—that we are asked to discuss this Bill while we are shut out from the information on the subject that we ought to have. Look at the present position of the Government as shown by their own admission. They admit that before we go into committee we ought to have the whole of the information we ask for before us. They admit that we have a right to know that the Government will proceed with the second measure immediately, and yet they say, although they know that the same process of debate can be repeated on going into committee as on the second reading, they will not give us the information

we require until, by reading the Bill a second time,
we have pledged ourselves to adopt the Bill, and until
they have got us into a corner. It has not been attempted yet—it is a task well worthy of the subtle
genius of the right honourable gentleman—to define
the relation of the information to this Bill, to show
that it is information so estranged and remote from
the principle of the Bill that it ought not to be laid
before us on the second reading, yet that it is so inti-
mately bound up and entwined with the principle of the
Bill that it must be laid before us and well considered
before we go into committee. I cannot, of course,
vouch for the truth of the rumour, because I think
Government have gone quite far enough in the way of
conceding things that are to be done after the second
reading, while maintaining their singular policy with
regard to what shall be done before the second reading, but I am told we are to have one more concession.
If we will only consent to give the Chancellor of the
Exchequer this victory over us by giving the Bill a
second reading, while we are utterly in the dark, to
please him, he will undertake that the two Bills shall
advance *pari passu*, and that one shall not be passed
without the other. This may meet some of the objections brought against the Bill, but it will not meet any
of the objections I have suggested. Would it show
you that you are properly treated by the Government?
—would it show that you are doing your duty to
the country and to your constituencies, in sanctioning

by your vote a measure the grounds and results of
which are studiously and purposely concealed from
you ? Would it show that you are acting in a manner
worthy of the dignity of this great assembly and of
the relations between this great assembly and the
executive Government, upon which the whole working power of our Constitution depends ? I refer to this,
because it is supposed that these things may be mentioned to us at the last moment, when it is too late to
reply to them. But I beg that you will consider
these questions before it is too late, and I am sure
that you will see that the statements, should they be
made, do not remove the real, solid objections to the
Bill. The noble lord the member for King's Lynn
argued with great force that the question of this proposed Redistribution Bill must come before a House
of Commons elected either by the present or by the
new constituency. In the first case, the House under
such circumstances would really be legislating with a
halter round its neck. The measure of its compliance
with the demands of the Government would be, not
what it might think right, but what it might believe
that the Parliament succeeding it would do. It would
cease to be a free agent, and would be placed in a
situation which I think no House not smitten with
a most inordinate love of life would wish to occupy.
The other alternative is, that the matter should be
decided by a House elected by the new constituency.
That will be a provisional constituency in which the

Government themselves profess no confidence, as they tell you that as soon as it is created they are going, by the redistribution of seats, to alter its numbers and electoral districts. The honourable gentleman the member for Westminster meets that argument of the noble lord by saying that he is contented with the Bill as it stands. He thinks that a sufficient answer, and member after member gets up and says the same thing. The question, however, is, not whether the honourable member is satisfied, but whether the Government is consistent. It is an argument against the Government that, if they thought this constituency was not fit to be a permanent one for the legislation of this country, it was monstrous to take such measures as would possibly throw the decision of this case into the hands of the very constituencies they had themselves treated as provisional and transitory. The argument of the noble lord is an *argumentum ad homines* as regards the Government, and is not addressed to the individual convictions of members.

I conclude that, on the clearest ground of self-respect, of what is due to the dignity and the honour of this House, and to the traditions of centuries entrusted to us, we ought never to allow—and I never will, as far as my vote goes—any Government to attempt anything of the kind. Besides the pleasure of the victory over the House of Commons, there is another motive—they want to get something they could not get if they disclosed the Seats Bill. We are not told what that something is, but we are furnished with the most pregnant grounds for conjecture, because it must be something so important that the Government prefers to stake its existence upon it rather than reveal it to the House of Commons. Every member who has the fortune to sit for a borough which is threatened by the Seats Bill, has a right to put the worst construction upon this measure. Besides, if it were only a little matter that lay behind, surely you cannot imagine Government going with their eyes open to what looks very like assured perdition, rather than let us know the details of the Redistribution Bill.

Having been headed off by the Government in my attempt to satisfy myself as to the question of the franchise, I might throw the matter up in despair; but, as I am anxious to pick up all the information I can, I will state what I know upon the subject. The main fault in my reasoning will be that it is not applicable to the future state of things, because that state of things is studiously concealed from us. It appears that the effect of this Bill, according to the figures of the Government, will be to introduce 144,000 7*l.* electors into the different boroughs, and the result will be that the working classes will have a majority in ninety-five boroughs, almost a majority in ninety-three, and more than one-third of the representation in eighty-five. This is mere matter of calculation, and an application of the rule of three sum we are asked to do. But then you must add to these figures 60,000 compound householders and non-ratepayers. You must take into consideration that the gross estimated rental is lower than the actual rental, that in thirty boroughs the Assessment Act has never come into operation at all, and that they contain one-half of the borough population. There is always a tendency in a progressive state of society for the actual rental to rise above the gross estimated rental, and therefore very considerable allowance must be made for that. Then there are a great many persons of the lodger class. All these things put together satisfy me that the majority of the 334 boroughs in England and Wales will be in the hands of the working classes immediately on the passing of the Bill. The argument of Mr. Baxter—not the member for Montrose, but a gentleman who has written a very excellent pamphlet upon the subject— shows a state of things well worthy of attention. He shows that, taking the three decades since the passing of the Reform Bill, the increase in the franchise was much more rapid in the first and least prosperous decade than in the other two. It increased 43 per cent. in the first decade, 27 in the second, and 20 in the third. Is not this a proof that the 10*l.* franchise eats up the 8*l.* and 9*l.*, which are drawn into the higher rate, while the higher fattens upon the spoil of its immediate inferiors in the world? And the same process will go on. The 7*l.* will eat up the 6*l.* and the 5*l.* The 7*l.* franchise is 2*s.* 9*d.* a week, and 2*s.* 6*d.* a week will give 6*l.* 10*s.* You see, therefore, how easy it is to ascend. The difference is merely one of threepence per week, and the margin is, consequently, very small. I am now only expressing my honest conviction on this matter. I cannot pretend to give it to the House upon complete evidence, because I have not the materials for demonstrating it to you. But that I have not those materials is not my own fault, but the fault of the Government, and, therefore, in considering this matter, it ought to weigh most strongly against them.

I now come to another subject, and that is the treatment of the House by the Government. Even before this House came into existence in its corporate capacity, the Chancellor of the Exchequer and the noble lord at the head of the Government set to work to devise its destruction, and the members of this House have been treated rather as condemned criminals than as friends in council. The right honourable gentleman in his opening speech forbore to give the House any reasons for bringing in this Bill. The policy of its introduction was challenged pretty warmly in the debate which took place at the time, but the Chancellor of the Exchequer forbore to reply. It was perfectly open to him to adopt that course, and to reserve his statement for the second reading. But what was the next thing? My noble friend the

member for Haddingtonshire (Lord Elcho)—to whom
the Government owe their idea of collecting statistics
—took the opportunity of asking, and not unreason-
ably, for some further information of the kind already
furnished by the Government. It was natural enough
that, having already information about the boroughs,
honourable members should desire to have similar
information about the counties. This consideration
was pressed upon the Chancellor of the Exchequer by
several honourable gentlemen, and he said, " You
" shall have no more statistics. Throw figures to the
" dogs—I'll none of them. Here you are speaking,
" measuring, calculating, as if the working classes
" were an invading army. Are they not your fellow-
" creatures ? Are they not fathers of families ? Are
" they not taxpayers ? Are they not your flesh and
" blood ? And do you capitulate and do you palter
" with them ? Here are statistics enough. Take
" that thine is and go thy way." I do not think that
the Chancellor of the Exchequer was very polite to
my noble friend, who, however, is well able to take
care of himself, or very respectful to the House. The
Government having furnished us this statistical information, ought certainly to be willing to listen to our
demands, because there is no possible reason why the
machinery by which the component parts of constituencies above 10l. were determined should not also
be employed to discover those below that figure.
This conduct throws light on the question of the

principle of the Bill, and appears to me to evince a
foregone conclusion on the part of the Government—
a determination that the thing was to be done at any
hazard, and a belief that the results were of no consequence whatever.   Then, again, it was not to us
that the Chancellor of the Exchequer imparted his
first impressions upon this matter.   He went to
Liverpool, and to an audience of a very different
character delivered those reasons for bringing in this
Bill which ought to have been laid before the House
on its first reading, in reply, or on the motion for its
second reading.   My right honourable friend should
have laid his reasons first of all before this House,
instead of imparting them to a select circle of friends
assembled in that most inappropriately named Philharmonic Hall at Liverpool.   And then the right
honourable gentleman and other members of the
Government, between the first and second reading,
and before the course which Parliament would adopt
with reference to the Bill was known, set on foot a
sort of ministerial agitation.   It is absurd to pretend
that the influence of agitation was not resorted to,
and it is not the fault of some of those who took part
in that agitation that it did not develope into an influence of terrorism.   Well, after these things were
over, the Chancellor of the Exchequer came back to
the House and favoured us with a languid *rechauffé*
of the arguments he had already employed at Liverpool, and thus the baked meats of the Philharmonic

Hall did coldly furnish forth the tables of the House of Commons. Well, Sir, I maintain, that from first to last, from the introduction of this measure to the present moment, the treatment we have received can only be regarded as an attempt to degrade and lower the character of the House of Commons. No doubt there are some gentlemen who do not view the matter in this light. They are probably accustomed to measures so much more drastic and more stringent, that they regard as matters of small consequence those lesser indignities which, nevertheless, do touch gentlemen and men of honour. I admit the Chancellor of the Exchequer has not written a letter asking the people to come down to this House, to fill the streets, and to hoot the members who are opposed to this Bill. I admit that he has not done a great many things of this kind, and therefore I would say with the honourable member for Westminster—

" ——-—— Habes pretium ——— ——
————— non pasces in cruce corvos,"

which I much prefer to

" Cruci non figeris."

Now, let us turn to the speech of the Chancellor of the Exchequer. I am in an unfortunate position. I am perfectly unable to argue the case with the Chancellor of the Exchequer, because when I try to argue with a man I seek for a common ground, and in the case of the Chancellor of the Exchequer I can find none. He argues in this way. Some people demand what fault is to be found in the existing state of things that it should be altered and destroyed. His reply is, " I am not bound to produce an indict-" ment." He does not say that any fault is to be found ; all he wishes to do is to make the House of Commons better, and to strengthen our institutions. But then he fails to show that the course he adopts will have that effect, nor has he, indeed, attempted at any time to prove anything of the kind. I drew out for him on a small scale, and, according to the best of my humble abilities, an estimate of the House of Commons, of its good and its bad qualities, and I challenged him to show how his proposed measure would diminish the evil and increase the good. The right honourable gentleman has taken no notice of that challenge, nor, indeed, has anybody attempted to meet it. He dare not, will not, put the matter upon this ground. I think the right honourable gentleman deliberately averted his eyes from the results in this matter, and, like the honourable member for Birming-ham, has determined to regard the question as a matter of justice, with which expediency, the good of the State, and the destiny of future ages, have nothing whatever to do. The right honourable gentleman says : —" I am not bound to produce an indictment. " People who say that a fault should be found before " a remedy is applied, assume that the franchise is " an evil, while I believe it is a good in itself." This

brings me back to the first of the two principles to
which I have alluded, and I do not think that I am
wrong in identifying the Chancellor of the Exchequer
with it. You will find that the same train of argument pervades the whole of his speech. The right
honourable gentleman says that we ought to give the
franchise to the 204,000 persons who will be affected
by this Bill, because they are our fellow-Christians.
But is that an argument for admitting them? Why,
Sir, who are the people in this country who do not
profess and call themselves Christians? It is an
argument, if anything, for the admission of the whole
of the male, and perhaps the female, population, but
it is no argument whatever for admitting the 204,000
more than anybody else. So, in the same way, with
the fathers of families, who are by no means peculiar
to the British nation. Then, again, with regard to
the taxpayers, or, as I should prefer to call them,
consumers of taxable commodities, which is a very
different thing. This class would include the whole of
our criminals, paupers, idiots, lunatics, children, and,
in fact, everybody else, and does not consist only of the
204,000 to whom this Bill refers. The argument
from flesh and blood applies not only to the human
race, but extends also to the animal kingdom, and, if
this principle were allowed, we might have another
" Beasts' Parliament," proposed after the pattern of
the assembly commemorated in the old epic of *Rey-
nard the Fox*. The right honourable gentleman then

maintains that it is a monstrous thing to exclude the
working classes, because their income amounts to
250,000,000*l*. But who are the people who enjoy
the income of 250,000,000*l*. ? Are they the 204,000
who are to receive the franchise ? If so, each of these
men would have 1200*l*. a year, and such an income
would effectually disqualify them from sharing in the
sympathy of the right honourable gentleman, because
they could then scarcely be regarded as belonging to
the working classes. What he means is, that these
250,000,000*l*. constitute the income of the whole of
the working classes ; but he doesn't propose to admit
the whole of the working classes. What I wish to
show, therefore, is, that this argument is good for
nothing at all, or it is good for extending the franchise to the whole of the people of the country. My
right honourable friend's argument about the contri-
butions to the revenue may be regarded in the same
light. He says that the working classes contribute
one-third or more of the revenue of this country ;
but who contribute it ? Then, again, the revenue
obtained from the working classes is chiefly derived
from the duties on tea and sugar, and on stimulants
—beer, spirits, and tobacco—and the revenue from
the latter source alone has of late years increased to
the enormous amount of 20,000,000*l*. But these
20,000,000*l*. are not contributed by the proposed
204,000 new voters. And so the thing comes round
again. It may possibly be quite right that the class

that only spends 1,260,000*l*. in 10*l*. houses, while the
duty on its expenditure on exciseable articles amounts
to a large part of 20,000,000*l*., should receive the
franchise. But then, it is an argument for the
admission of the whole class, and not of any particular portion. The House will, I think, see that
I am not wasting their time in referring to these
matters. I want to show that this measure is not
founded upon any calculation of results, but upon
broad sweeping principles, having their rise in the
assumed rights of man and other figments of that
kind, which, if admitted, do not prove that the
present measure is a good one, but that what is
needed is universal suffrage. And that is a point of
view in which, being denied the information we
ought to have, we are bound, in duty to ourselves and
to our country, to regard it. We have been asked
whether it is to be believed that the political limit of
10*l*. is to exist for ever; and, I ask, whether the same
thing cannot be said for the 7*l*. figure as well as for
the other? We had from the honourable member
for Birmingham, on the first reading of this Bill, a
specimen of the ruinous logic by which these things
are to be accomplished. He took his stand upon the
fact of some right honourable gentleman opposite
having been once in favour of an 8*l*. franchise, and
he said, "We want a 7*l*. franchise, so that there is
"only a pound between us, and you won't fall out
"with me for a pound." So the Constitution is

knocked down to the lowest bidder. I won't fall out
with the honourable member for Birmingham.   I
would give him a pound out of my own pocket, if
he wanted it; but his pound is no joke. The honourable member for Birmingham's pound means 100,000
men, and 100,000 men of whom he may know a
great deal, but of whom we—instructed in the matter
only from what we learn by public documents—know
nothing at all. Parenthetically I may observe that
I should be very much obliged to the honourable
member for Birmingham if he would make his
soliloquies a little less dramatic. The Chancellor of
the Exchequer asks, "Is it to be tolerated that in
"this country we are to have a narrow precinct called
"the Constitution, within which we have gathered
"some million, or 1,200,000 or 1,300,000, while out-
"side of it we have some four-and-a-half millions?"
But I want to know whether, after we have admitted
within the precinct some 200,000 or 300,000 of these
outsiders, the proportion of numbers upon which the
right honourable gentleman bases his argument is in
any sensible degree diminished. If the argument is
good for anything, it goes in not for the few hundred
thousand only, but for the 4,500,000. There might
have been some answer to this if the right honourable
gentleman had shown us in the speeches which he
has delivered, either in the House or to the people at
Liverpool, the least qualification for this principle,
what limit he puts upon it, or why 7l., or any other

limit, should be thought of, or how he reconciles it,
or how he thinks the thing will fit in with the state
of our society. But he has done nothing of the kind.
It is a principle the most dangerous, the most sweeping, the most democratic, that has ever been set
forth by any Minister in this House. He has taken
it without modification and without qualification—
not to work upon our minds—for I trust there are
very few educated gentlemen upon whom such views
as these would make any impression whatever, but to
work upon the minds of the people at large, who have
not had the advantage of the culture which we have
enjoyed. Then there is another point. We have
been, it seems, during the last few years, doing something for the working classes—and here the right
honourable gentleman is exceedingly patronising—we
have done a good deal for their education, the clergy
have done a great deal for their morals, and something has been done for them in sanitary matters ;—
is it to be supposed that, after all this has been done,
the franchise should not be extended to them ? The
right honourable gentleman does not point to any
tangible result from all this, to show that there is
any reason in point of fitness for admitting them to
the franchise by lowering it. He merely asserts,
" You have done all this for them ; it must have pro-
" duced a result ;" he assumes that the result was good
and sufficient, and he calls on you to lower the franchise
accordingly. I say, if he proved that the result was

K

good and sufficient, which he does not pretend to do, it
would not be an argument for lowering the franchise
unless he could also show that the lowering of the
franchise was on the whole likely to work for the
good of society. He does not even satisfy his own
condition ; for he asks us to admit people of whom
he knows nothing, except that they contribute to the
revenue, have a large aggregate income, and have
had a good deal of money spent upon them by the
Government in order to improve their condition ; and
then, speaking in a patronising manner, he says,
" We have done a good deal for them, so now, let us
"make them our masters." With affected ignorance,
the right honourable gentleman says, "if Democracy
" be liberty, we have no occasion to be afraid ; but if
" Democracy be vice and ignorance, then this Govern-
"ment is not democratic." Who ever said it was?
The question is, not whether this Government is
democratic, but whether the Government he asks us
to make must not necessarily be democratic. Does
not the right honourable gentleman know what
Democracy is? Whatever we learnt at Oxford, we
learnt that Democracy was a form of government in
which the poor, being many, governed the whole
country, including the rich, who were few, and for
the benefit of the poor. The question is—Is not that
the form of government which the right honourable
gentleman is seeking to introduce? It is not, then,
liberty or vice ; it is the government of the rich

by the poor. Why shouldn't we call it by its right
name at once ? That is a very short, but, for my
purpose, a sufficient analysis of the argument of
the Chancellor of the Exchequer at Liverpool, because I don't pretend in the least to answer it. I
simply deny that justice has anything to do with the
matter; it is purely a question of State policy. We
are told that we are bound to forge our own fetters,
while we shut our eyes to the consequences of what
we do; but the essence of my theory is, that you are
bound to look most strictly to the results we may
reasonably anticipate. From the sweeping nature of
this Bill, when carefully looked at, from the manner
in which it has been forced upon the House, and
from the arguments by which it has been supported
by the right honourable gentleman, I maintain that
it is founded upon the principles I have mentioned,
and I may state, that not one person who has spoken
on it in connection with the Government, has taken a
view of it different from his, or has endeavoured in
the least to qualify the principle upon which it is
based ; and that is that the franchise is due to every
one whom you cannot show to be unfit. But that
principle followed up leads straight to ruin ; it asserts
that the franchise is a thing we are bound to pay ;
and so clear is our obligation, that we are desired
to shut our eyes and disregard all expediency, and to
leave the constituencies so created to take care of us
and of themselves. We are told that we are under

no more obligation to see what use they would make
of the franchise than we are to inquire what use a
creditor would make of a payment of money justly
due to him.   Anything more dangerous, more utterly
subversive, I cannot conceive.   We must also keep in
sight the democratic influence of the redistribution of
seats, whatever it may be.

If the House will bear with me, I will call attention to another matter.   My honourable friend the
member for Westminster, has come out in a new
character.   I do not speak of the excellent speech
which he has made, because, having known him
for many years, I was quite sure that, when he took
the trouble to give us his best thoughts, instead
of dealing in impromptus, those great abilities which
are acknowledged to be his would be apparent.
But my honourable friend has taken a new stand.
He has taken many positions with regard to this subject, as those who are acquainted with his works well
know ; but he has now come forward in the capacity
of the advocate of my second principle, the doctrine
of class representation.   He demands the franchise
for the working classes ; because he says they are not
sufficiently represented now, although they have a
fourth of the votes in boroughs.   He offers no argument in support of his assertion ; I therefore pass it
by, as I wish to deal with arguments and not
assertions.   My honourable friend does say, however,
that the working class have not so much influence

as they might be supposed to have, because they are
so distributed that they are usually out-voted; and
thus they are in a position little better than if they
had no votes at all. He regrets, on their behalf, that
some law is not in force for giving to minorities
representation. I believe that is a fair statement of
my honourable friend's argument. [Mr. Mill was understood to assent.] Now, I think my honourable
friend ought, in passing, to have adverted to the
argument which I have so frequently insisted upon
in this House—namely, that if the working classes
have only 128,000 in the present constituencies,
it is very much their own fault, because many more
of them have the means, if they choose to live in 10*l.*
houses. The law, therefore, is not to blame in this
respect. He might have adverted to a case which I
may mention as the type of many others. The
Southwick glass manufactory at Sunderland, is a
large establishment where many workmen are employed, earning from 4*l.* to 5*l.* a-week. It is complained that none of these persons had the franchise.
But whose fault is that? These workmen are earning, some 200*l.* and some 250*l.* a year, and yet they
live in houses under 10*l.* a-year in value. Is it
the fault of the law? Of course, I must not say
whose fault it is. Every gentleman is free to say
anything that is complimentary of the working
classes in general and his own constituency in particular; but any gentleman who says anything in

the slightest degree not pleasing to them is thought
to have grossly misconducted himself.   But now,
having adopted the theory of classes, we cannot, as
my honourable friend was inclined to do, take it up in
order to make an argument in favour of the working
classes, and lay it down when it makes against them.
His logical mind will tell him that he must follow
the principle out to its legitimate conclusions, and so
he is bound to show us that the extension of the
franchise which he asks for the working classes,
though a wide extension, can be given without
injury to the other classes.   He must not take the
theory up for the working classes alone, but for
all classes.   Now, he has not condescended to show
us how the extension which he approves would influence the position of any other class except the working class, or rather the poor class, for I view this
question not as one between working classes and
those who employ them, but between those who have
property and those who have not.   Now, Sir, I would
refer my honourable friend and the House, to the
preface of the third edition of his work on " Political
Economy."   It was published in 1852, so that my
honourable friend has had time to change his mind
since, and he is entitled to do it.   This is what he
said.   I am very glad that I didn't :—

" The only objection to which any great import-
" ance will be found to be attached in the present
" edition, is the unprepared state of mankind in

" general, and of the labouring classes in particular;
" their extreme unfitness at present for any order of
" things which would make any considerable demand
" on either their intellect or their virtue."

That was in 1852 ; but we have the opinion of my
honourable friend in 1861. In his work on " Representative Government," he says :—

" I regard it as wholly inadmissible that any person
" should participate in the suffrage without being
" able to read, write, and, I will add, perform the
" common operations of arithmetic. Universal teach-
" ing must precede universal enfranchisement. No
" one, but those in whom an *à priori* theory has
" silenced common sense, will maintain that power
" over others, over the whole community, should be
" given to people who have not acquired the com-
" monest and most essential requisites for taking care
" of themselves."

My honourable friend himself cheers those remarks.
I hope he will take some opportunity of telling us
what is the process of investigation he entered on for
the purpose of satisfying himself that the electors in
7*l.* houses will be found prepared for the exercise of
the franchise. I hope he will tell us what evidence he
has to produce of their intellect and their virtue. I
hope he will satisfy us, if he has satisfied himself, of
their being able to read and write and to perform all
the common operations of arithmetic, including, I suppose—though he did not state it in that passage—the

rule of three. I hope he has satisfied himself that universal teaching has preceded universal enfranchisement. Of course the word "universal" might be struck out and the sense would remain the same —namely, that instruction must precede enfranchisement. I hope he will show us how he has satisfied himself that those persons whom he proposes to enfranchise—to whom he would intrust the interests of others—are persons who have acquired the commonest and most essential requisites for taking care of themselves. If not, how can he reconcile his present position with any principle, but that *à priori* theory of which he speaks? I don't say my honourable friend can't do it. He can do most things, and perhaps he can do this; but I only say, as things stand, he has not done it, and that his own writings are against the principle which he now supports by his speech. My honourable friend half took up the challenge which I threw out when I asked in what this Parliament—which has only just come into existence, and which was condemned before it was born—has been found wanting. He pointed out our old friend the cattle plague. I am not going to argue that question over again ; but my honourable friend said, that if the working classes had been represented here, they might have objected to persons being twice compensated for their cattle. Now, Sir, I cannot persuade my honourable friend, but I think, if I had the working men here, I could show them that the persons to whom

the honourable member for Westminster alludes will
not be compensated twice. Suppose a farmer has
100 head of cattle, which are killed to prevent the
spread of the disease. He is compensated at less
than their value, and then it becomes necessary for
agricultural purposes that he should go into the
market and buy another 100 head of cattle. The
loss which he sustains is not only the difference
between the value of his former cattle and the compensation which he got for them, but also the amount
by which the price of cattle has been enhanced by the
disease, and enhanced in some degree by the slaughter. I cannot persuade my honourable friend, because
he is a philosopher, but I think I could persuade the
working men whom he seeks to bring among us, that
so far from being paid twice over, the farmer in that
case has never been paid once. You can put a case
which will be the other way. If a man has a large
herd of cattle and is compensated for a few of them,
he may be paid over again by the enhanced prices of
the remainder. You can put the case both ways;
but what I complain of is the narrowness and illiberality of saying that this is a matter which cannot
admit of two aspects—that those who differ from my
honourable friend must be wrong, and that if it were
not for the faulty constitution of this House, we should
see and judge things in the same manner as he does.

Mr. MILL said—I wish to correct the last assertion
of my right honourable friend. I never imputed to

honourable gentlemen in this House, or to the landed interest, that they were wilfully wrong.

MR. LOWE.—I may remark that I suppose no one in this House would have any objection to working men coming here, if the constituencies wished to send them. They can do so now if they like, and, therefore, we need not take up time in arguing the point, because I am sure, that whenever the constituencies may think proper to send working men here, we shall receive those representatives properly, and listen to them with respect. But my honourable friend told us of the subjects which the working classes might wish to debate here. He referred to " the " right of labour." That sounds very like the right " to " labour, of which we heard in 1848. Are we to have the doctrines of Fourier and St. Simon discussed here? We are told that in so doing we shall educate the working man. I protest against this. We are here to legislate for this country, and if we look after the Executive Government pretty sharply—if we take care of our finance, and if we watch the Foreign Office, we shall be doing better than we should do by converting this House into an academy or a gymnasium for the instruction even of the *élite* of the working classes. My honourable friend said that if the working classes were here they would establish a school in every parish in a very few years. Well, that is a subject on which I ought to know something; and I may say that the main object I had in view, in the changes which I proposed on the part of the Government in the education system, was to benefit the working classes. Under the old system the poor children were not properly taught. The upper children, the children of richer parents, were examined, and the money was paid ; but the lower and poorer children were neglected. The upper children had generally had some education at home ; but the poor children had received no education at home, and they were not done justice to in the schools. The object of the Revised Code was to insure that education should be given to the poor just as' much as to the rich ; so that the object was one mainly—indeed, entirely—for the working classes. But in that object I never received the slightest assistance in any way from the working classes. The opposition to it was very much from the members for the large towns in which the working classes form a considerable portion of the constituencies ; but the working classes themselves never interfered in the matter. They did not care about it. The school-masters interfered, and got members of Parliament to oppose the code ; but the working classes never entered into the matter at all. How, therefore, my honourable friend can think that working men will deal with this question, in which they have never shown any interest, and which is very intricate and difficult, I cannot understand. Again, my honourable friend ought to be prepared to show how he means to resist the course of what he calls false democracy. If the working classes, in addition to being a majority in the boroughs, get a redistribution of the seats in their favour, it will follow that their influence will be enormously increased. They will then urge the House of Commons to pass another Franchise Bill, and another Redistribution Bill to follow it. Not satisfied with these, yet another Franchise Bill and another redistribution of seats will, perhaps, follow. It will be a ruinous game of see-saw. No one can tell where it will stop, and it will not be likely to stop until we get equal electoral districts and a qualification so low that it will keep out nobody.

There is another matter with which my honourable friend has not dealt : I mean the point of combination among the working classes. To many persons, there appears great danger that the machinery which at present exists for strikes and trade unions may be used for political purposes. And that this use of such machinery has not escaped the attention of thinking men, I will show you, from a speech made by the honourable member for Birmingham, in January, 1860. In that speech he said :

" Working men have associations ; they can get up " formidable strikes against capital—sometimes for " things that are just, sometimes for things that are " impossible. They have associations, trade societies, " organizations, and I want to ask them why it is " that all these various organizations throughout the

" country could not be made use of for the purpose of
" obtaining their political rights ?"

Why is it that those various organizations have not
been so made use of? The honourable gentleman
asked that question in 1860, and I admit that hitherto
he has received no answer. Why? I will tell you
why. The working classes, to use his own expression,
are the lever. But they must have a fulcrum before
they can act. They have not got it. Give them the
majority of the voters in a number of boroughs, and
it is supplied to them. It is not by passing resolutions and making speeches they coerce their masters.
They watch their opportunity ; they wait for the time
when large orders are in, and they refuse to work,
that is the fulcrum they work on. Give them the
majority of voters—that will be their political fulcrum ; and if the honourable gentleman repeats his
advice, no doubt they will use it with avidity. I
want to call the attention of the House, in a few
words, to the condition of the trade unions, because
we are all anxious to discover, if we can, the future
of that Democracy which, I believe, this Bill will be
the first means of establishing. I take one class, the
operative stonemasons—a very influential association,
numbering 80,000 members, and having a large
capital. Last year, after a strike of nineteen weeks,
this body of masons beat the masters. Let me call
the attention of the House to a letter which they
sent to the employers :

"We present you with the wishes of our trade
" union, requesting a reply on or before Saturday
" next:—Mr. Thomas and all non-society plasterers
" to be discharged; all non-society carpenters and
" improvers to be discharged; piecework to be abo-
" lished, &c.   On behalf of the United Building
" Trades, JOHN BRAY, Chairman."

Mark what that is.   See the power unions have of
drawing men within their own circle.   You say, if
they become political bodies, men who want to have
nothing to do with politics will have nothing to do
with them.   Can they help themselves?   They will
be overborne, overawed; they are like men contend-
ing with a mäelstrom into which, struggle as they
may, eventually they will be sucked.   This is a para-
graph which I have taken from an Edinburgh paper:

" The tailors' strike may now be considered at an
" end, the men having agreed to accept the London
" 'log,' with payment at the rate of 5½d. an hour, as
" offered by the masters.   These terms the men seem
" to consider as highly satisfactory, entailing, as they
" will, an increase of from 15 to 25 per cent. on their
" wages.   We have been informed that the men have
" made it a condition with the masters that the ' black
" sheep,' or those who have continued working during
" the lock-out, shall not obtain employment until they
" become members of the society, besides paying a
" fine of 10s. each."

You will say these men do not want to join these

societies—I dare say they don't; but what choice
have they? The truth is—and of this I want to
convince the House—that these trades unions are far
more unions against the best, the most skilful, the
most industrious, and most capable of the labourers
themselves, than they are against their masters.
Listen to another rule which is taken from the
printed book of the co-operative society of masons :

" Working overtime, tending to our general injury
" by keeping members out of employment, shall be
" abolished, excepting in case of accident or necessity."

This is your future political organization. Again:

" It is also requested that lodges harassed by piece-
" work or sub-contracting, do apply at a reasonable
" time for a grant to abolish it."

That is to say, men are first to be driven into these
unions by pressure such as I have explained to the
House, and then, once they are got within the limits,
whatever their necessities, whatever the pressure of
their families, they are not to be allowed to eke out
their income by working overtime. To do so might
enable a man, a poor man, to raise himself out of
that sphere of life, and furnish him with some still
better occupation. But although his good conduct
may have invited the confidence and attracted the
notice of his master, he is not to be allowed to take
a sub-contract, to make a little money in that way.
The object of all these proceedings is obvious. It is
to enclose as many men as can be got into these

societies, and then to apply to them the strictest democratic principle, and that is, to make war against all superiority, to keep down skill, industry, and capacity, and make them the slaves of clumsiness, idleness, and ignorance. One extract more, and I have done:

"In localities where that most obnoxious and de-
" structive system generally known as ' chasing ' is
" persisted in, lodges should use every effort to put
" it down. Not to take less time than that taken by
" an average mason in the execution of the first por-
" tion of each description of work, is the practice that
" should be adopted among us as much as possible ;
" and where it is plainly visible that any member or
" other individual is striving to overwork or ' chase '
" his fellow-workmen, thereby acting in a manner
" calculated to lead to the discharge of members, or a
" reduction of their wages, the party so acting shall
" be summoned before the lodge, and if the charge
" be satisfactorily proved, a fine shall be inflicted on
" the party implicated."

That is to say, when a poor workman, naturally quicker and more skilful than those about him, and with a wish to distinguish himself, shows his capacity, so as to oblige his fellow-workmen to exert themselves more than goes to what they please to call the time taken by an average mason in the execution of his work, he is to be fined and put down. Add to this—what does not appear in any of the rules and regulations, but what we know well—the system of terrorism that lurks behind these trades' unions, and makes the lives of the "knob-sticks" and "black sheep" miserable till they are driven into them. And then look at this tremendous' machinery; if you only arm it with the one thing it wants—the Parliamentary vote!

It remains for us to consider—and I am sure the House will be glad to hear that this is the last branch of the subject which I shall have to treat—the results of the step that you are invited to take. I assume that this is really a very large and sweeping change in the democratic direction, giving, as I believe, the majority of votes in boroughs to the working classes. On that point we are compelled to differ, because the Government will not give us the materials necessary for making an accurate calculation. This change is to be followed by a further and very large change in the redistribution of seats. It does not depend upon any Government, upon any Minister, perhaps upon any House of Commons, to say where those changes will stop. One honourable member speaks of this as a change that will last fifty years. He has put the matter as entirely out of his power as a man who, rolling a stone down the side of a mountain, fixes beforehand in his own mind the time it will take to reach the bottom. We have had this matter put before us from one very peculiar and invidious point of view. It seems to have been thought that the

L

manner to discuss the probable result of a great democratic change in this country was, on the one side, to praise the working men, especially those among our own constituents, and, on the other, to remain silent, because nothing except praise, it is presumed, would be borne. I think that is not the way to approach this question. There is considerable risk that in this way the basis of our institutions may be complimented away. We are rich in experience on this subject. We have the experience of our own state and condition, which, compared with that of other countries, may be called a stationary state; we have the experience of our colonies all over the world, which may be described as in a transition state; and we have the experience of those two great democracies, France and America, where Democracy may be said to have run its course and arrived at something like its ultimate limits. It is inexcusable in us if we do not apply our minds to the consideration of this subject, and draw from this rich field of observation conclusions more trustworthy and more reliable than those to be gained from our own isolated experience, particularly as this is so often contradictory. The honourable gentleman the Under-Secretary for the Colonies began his speech the other night by telling us, that if the working men had a fault in the world, it was their too great reverence for authority, and then he went on to tell us, that if we did not accede to their present moderate requests, it would

be a question, not of how much we should give, but
of how much they would take. That was the sum of
the honourable gentleman's remarks; he told us that
the burden of proof would be effectually shifted, and
he said, what we all understood the Chancellor of the
Exchequer to say before he wrote his preface and
made his two speeches to explain away his meaning.
The working men entered the honourable gentleman
the Under-Secretary's speech like lambs, and they
left it as lions; and so his estimate of them may be
taken to answer itself. The question of peace or war
has been a good deal touched upon in this debate.
The Chancellor of the Exchequer, at Liverpool, was
very much struck with the magnificent spectacle of
the strength put forth by Democracy in the recent
war. I would rather he had commended it for something which it had done in peace. I never doubted
that Democracy was a terrible warlike power. It is
not the educated and reflective who are influenced
by ideas, but the half educated and the unreflective;
and if you show to the ignorant, and poor, and half
educated wrong, injustice, and wickedness anywhere,
their generous instincts rise within them, and nothing
is easier than to get up a cry for the redress of those
grievances. We feel the injustice, too; but we look
not merely at the injustice itself—we look before and
after, we look at the collateral circumstances, at what
must happen to trade, revenue, and our own position
in the world, and we look also at what must happen

to those very poor persons themselves before we commit ourselves to a decided course. Persons, also, who have something to lose are less anxious to lose it than those who have little at stake often, even though these last may by the loss be reduced to absolute poverty. At the time of the Crimean war we actually got up an enthusiasm on behalf of that most abominable and decrepit despotism—the Turkish empire. Nothing would have been more popular in England than a war on behalf of Hungary in 1849, or one lately on behalf of Poland. Wherever cruelty or injustice exists, the feelings of the humbler class of Englishmen—to their honour be it said—revolt against it, and, not possessing the quality of circumspection, their impulse is to go straight at the wrong and redress it, without regard to ulterior consequences. Therefore, to suggest that in making the institutions of the country more democratic we have any security from war, that we do not greatly increase the risk of war, seems to me supremely ridiculous. What is taking place in the Australian colonies? Victoria and New South Wales are both governed by universal suffrage, and it is as much as we can do to prevent their going to war with each other. Look at America. A section of the American Democracy revolted and broke up the Union, the rest fought to preserve it; the war was fought out to the bitter end, and now that the war is concluded they are almost ready to go to war again to prevent the doing of that which they took up arms to accomplish. Look at free trade. If we have a precious jewel in the world, it is our free trade policy. It has been everything to us. With what eyes do Democracies look at it? Let us turn to history, and not enter into particular cases of particular working men. Take the facts. Canada has raised her duties enormously, and justified them upon protectionist principles. The Prime Minister of New South Wales, at this moment is a strong protectionist. The Ministry in Victoria were freetraders, but by the will of the people they have been converted, and have become protectionists. So vigorously has the question been fought that destruction is threatened to the second branch of the Legislature, though equal in power to the other, in defiance of the laws of the country, and all to carry out a policy of protection. Then we come to America. America out-protects protection—there never was anything like the zeal for protection in America. With a revenue that needs recruiting, by every means in their power they persist in sacrificing the most valuable resources; with a frontier that bids defiance to any effectual attempts to guard it, they persist in maintaining duties that provoke to wholesale smuggling rather than reduce them by a single penny. And, as if anxious at once to illustrate the free-trade and peace proclivities of Democracy, they terminate the treaty with Canada, which was a step in the direction of free trade, and then seek to enforce by violence the very rights which the treaty they have put an end to secured. I will add one word as to Communism. The honourable member for Lambeth has certainly furnished us with a very good argument in favour of the proposition of having working men to represent themselves. He has drawn such a picture of them as they would scarcely have given of themselves. What does he say? He says, in the first place, that they are entirely unable to understand that wages depend on the laws of supply and demand; that, he says, is entirely out of their conception. Then he tells us that they have no conception of any difference between the remuneration of the labour of the strong and the weak; the strong are to work for the weak, and all are to be paid alike. Then, as far as Government is concerned, the working men—so far from having a horror of a paternal and interfering Government — want us to prevent their going to public-houses, and this in the name of universal liberty, equality, and fraternity! Not only so, but they insist that the money of their fellow-taxpayers ought to be spent in building houses for them to live in, because it is not for them, forsooth, to appropriate a sufficient proportion of their own incomes to pay the amount of rent required to accomplish this object on commercial principles.

I come now to the question of the representatives of the working classes. It is an old observation that every Democracy is in some respects similar to a

Despotism. As courtiers and flatterers are worse
than despots themselves, so those who flatter and
fawn upon the people are generally very inferior to
the people, the objects of their flattery and adulation.
We see in America, where the people have undis-
puted power, that they do not send honest, hard-
working men to represent them in the Congress, but
traffickers in office, bankrupts, men who have lost
their character and been driven from every respectable way of life, and who take up politics as a last
resource. There is one subject of immense importance
to a constitutional House—viz., the expenses of elections. The member for Westminster thinks this Bill
will abridge the influence of wealth. Will it do so?
Let us see. Those expenses are of two kinds,—
legitimate and illegitimate. The Bill now before
the House will enormously increase the electoral
districts, and in many it will double, and in some
treble, the legitimate expenses of elections. I am
speaking among people who are thoroughly acquainted
with this subject, and they know too well that the
expenses of elections depend as much on the illegitimate as on the legitimate agencies employed.
Can it be argued, then, that by admitting occupiers
of houses between 10*l.* and 7*l.*, you will diminish the
illegitimate expenses of elections? Yes, it can, for
it has been thus argued by the right honourable gentleman the President of the Board of Trade. The
right honourable gentleman—and I am happy to have

his authority—says—mind, I do not—that the people
in a great many of the boroughs are very corrupt.

MR. MILNER GIBSON.—I said "some voters."

MR. LOWE.—Well, some voters in some boroughs.
I wish to be cautious. Some of these voters have
political opinions, but their minds are so sluggish that
they cannot be influenced without a certain *lene tor-
mentum* or reminder in the shape of a five-pound note;
while others, who have no political opinions, are slow
and procrastinating, being never able to make up
their minds until about 3 o'clock on the day of the
poll, when by some inscrutable influence they are
urged on to a little activity. Others are judicial, and
cannot decide till they have been paid on both sides.
It is said, here's a disease, cure it, dilute its poison by
admitting a large number to the franchise. Well,
that would be a very good argument, if health was
catching as well as disease. If I had half-a-dozen
diseased cattle, and I turned one hundred sound
cattle among them, I might infect the new ones, but
I do not think that I should do much good to the sick
ones. And now let me say that I have never been
answered as to the effect which the lowering of the
franchise would have upon this House, and I suppose
that I never shall be. One great mistake is made—
it is almost a childish oversight—and that is to speak
of this House as if it were merely a legislative body.
The members of this House have a position, a consideration, and a weight in this country such as no

legislative body ever had in any country in the world. This is not because of any extraordinary skill in legislation; we have other functions. The House is the administrator of the public funds, but, besides that, it is a main part of the Executive Government of the country. It can unmake the executive, and it can go a long way to make it. It is, therefore, well to consider that you are dealing with a Legislature entirely different from either the Assembly of France or the Congress of America. We all know that while our legislation has been more vigorous and better since the Reform Bill, the Executive Government has shown weakness and languor. If you exaggerate, if you intensify the causes already at work, you will find it necessary to do what has been done elsewhere —to separate the functions of the Executive Government from the House of Commons altogether, to break up that most salutary union which exists between them, and to have a Government which shall not depend for its existence upon a majority in this House. Now, that is a consideration the seriousness of which it is perfectly impossible to exaggerate. In the colonies, they have got democratic assemblies. And what is the result? Why, responsible government becomes a curse, instead of a blessing. In Australia there is no greater evil to the stability of society, to industry, to property, and to the well-being of the country, than the constant change which is taking place in the Government, and the uncertainty that it creates, and the pitting of rival factions against each other. The same thing, I think, is wonderfully exemplified in Victoria, where you have a Government which is now under the influence of universal suffrage, and which is at war at once with the judicial authorities and the Upper Chamber, because neither will yield to its illegal exactions. The Supreme Court decides against the levy of taxes by resolutions of the Assembly, and the Government dissolves Parliament and appeals to universal suffrage against the decision of the Supreme Court. What does this tend to? It tends to anarchy, and from that anarchy these colonies must be relieved. They can, however, only be relieved by depriving them of that boon which in an unfortunate hour they received —that of responsible government coupled with universal suffrage—and by placing their Government in some permanent hands, so that the executive shall not be in a perpetual state of change. Look a little farther, and see what happened in France, where there was a limited constituency in the time of Louis Philippe, and Parliamentary government until the revolution of 1848. Then came the Assembly elected by universal suffrage, and still with a responsible Government. But that responsible Government became weaker every day until the *coup d'état*, and 1 doubt if there are many gentlemen here who could tell me the name of the nominal Premier under whom the liberties of France were overthrown. The great men who founded the Constitution of America foresaw this, and they took means to obviate the difficulty. They knew perfectly well in what the enormous advantage of our system of government consisted. They knew that Democracy required checks, and they sought to check it by various means. They, in fact, checked Democracy with Democracy, and elected a President. They added, too, what we have not got—the principle of federalism, which resisted the downward tendency of Democracy by a lateral pressure. To use a familiar illustration, they held a piece of coal up by a pair of tongs. That has been the course adopted in America. And now let us see what has come of it. They have fought out a civil war, and gained a great victory. But we must remember that men's opinions were divided. One side wanted to prevent the South from regaining the power it possessed before the civil war, and the other to reconstruct the Union on the principle of State rights. In this country, the question would be decided by a vote displacing or retaining the Government; and those who were displaced would carry into the wilderness their offences, as the scapegoat carried off the offences of the people of Israel. But mark what happens in America. You cannot get rid of the President, who sits for four years; nor the Congress, which sits for two years. Therefore, you have an internecine duel, and those who ought to combine and coalesce for the good of the country are in factious opposition. The whole frame of the Con-

stitution is thus stretched till it cracks—to try, not who
shall hold the supreme power, but which of the two
rival institutions shall gain the victory over the other.
You have seen senators expelled in order to secure a
majority of two-thirds, and things have arrived at
such a pitch that no man need be surprised at seeing
a second civil war, from the inability of the Constitution to solve the difficulty in which the first civil
war had placed the country. Let us apply this to
our own country. We have in our Government an
invaluable institution, and let us not rashly or fool-
ishly put it in peril. I do not know whether honourable gentlemen have read the report of the debate
which took place the other day in the French
Chamber, between M. Thiers and M. Rouher, on
the subject of the introduction into France of a
responsible Government. Though my sympathies, as
an Englishman, are with M. Thiers, I confess that in
my opinion the argument of M. Rouher was un-
answerable, for the question was, whether responsible
government could co-exist with universal suffrage?
If you were to have responsible government back,
said M. Rouher, you must also have back the *pays
legal*, the old constituencies containing 200,000 voters,
for, without that, he argued, M. Thiers was asking
for a thing without being prepared to realize the only
conditions under which it could exist.

Now, Sir, Democracy has yet another tendency,
which it is worth while to study at the present

moment. It is singularly prone to the concentration of power. Under it individual men are small, and the Government is great. That must be the character of a Government which represents the majority, and which absolutely tramples down and equalizes everything except itself. And Democracy has another strong peculiarity. It looks with the utmost hostility on all institutions not of immediate popular origin, which intervene between the people and the sovereign power which the people have set up. To use the words of the right honourable gentleman the Chancellor of the Duchy of Lancaster, it likes to have everything as representative as possible, and that which is not representative it likes to have swept away. Now, look what was done in France. Democracy has left nothing in that country between the people and the Emperor, except a bureaucracy which the Emperor himself has created. In America it has done almost the same thing. You have there nothing to break the shock between the two great powers of the State. The wise men who framed the Constitution tried to provide a remedy by dividing functions as much as possible. They assigned one function to the President, another to the Senate, a third to the Congress, and a fourth to the different States. But all their efforts have been in vain, and you see how two hostile camps have arisen, and the terrible duel which is now taking place between them. Now, apply that to England, which, above

all countries in the world, is the country of inter-
mediate institutions.   There are between the people
and the throne a vast number of institutions which
our ancestors have created.   Their principle in creating
them seems to have been this—that they looked a
great deal to liberty and very little to equality.   If
there were something to be done, they sought for
some existing institution which was able to do it.   If
some change were required, they altered things as
little as they could, and were content to go on in
that manner.   This is a country of privileges above
all other countries, but the privileges have been given,
not as in other countries—as in France before the
Revolution, for instance—for the benefit of the privileged classes, but because our ancestors, in all moderation, believed this to be the best way to insure
order, and good government and stability.   It may
be difficult to prove upon theory how all this should
be, because ancient governments, as Burke finely
remarks, are seldom based on abstract principles,
but rather are the materials from which abstract
principles are drawn.   I think we should act more
wisely and more worthily to the country, if we were to
ascertain what lessons of wisdom may be drawn from
the signal success of our own Government, instead of
trying to borrow from the people of America notions
which lead to such results as I have been endeavouring to depict.   But, Sir, have we succeeded?   I will
quote, not my own words, but an unexceptionable

witness. "It has been our privilege," says the speaker whom I quote, "to see a process going forward in "which the throne has acquired broader and deeper "foundations in the affections of the country; in which "the law has commended itself more and more to the "respect and attachment of the people; in which the "various classes of the community have come into close "communion, the one with the other; in which the "great masses of our labouring fellow-countrymen have "come to be better supplied than they were in the "time of their immediate forefathers, and in which, "upon the whole, a man desirous of the welfare of his "kind, looking out on the broad surface of society, "may thank his God, and say, 'Behold, how good and "· pleasant a thing it is for brethren to dwell together "'in unity!'" Well, those eloquent words were the words of the Chancellor of the Exchequer, and they were spoken on the 14th of September last, just two months before he began the concoction of the Bill, which has been so very successful in illustrating the manner in which brethren dwell together in unity. Now, let us suppose Democracy to be established in a greater or less degree in this country. With what eyes would it look upon the institutions which I have alluded to? What would be the relation of this House with the House of Peers? I will call a witness. Eight years ago the honourable member for Birmingham inverted his present process. He is now anxious to secure means; he was then proclaiming

ends.   He said then, " See what I will do for you, if
" you will only give me Reform ;" but now he says,
" Give me Reform, and be assured that I will do
" nothing." But the Bill does not say that.   The
words he uttered eight years ago remain.   They have
never been retracted, and I have no reason to suppose that the honourable gentleman wishes to retract,
or is ashamed of any one of them.   The honourable
gentleman said on one occasion—I am speaking from
memory; but, though I am not sure about the words,
I am about the meaning which the honourable
gentleman intended to convey—that, as far as the
House of Peers was concerned, he did not believe
that even the Peers themselves could suppose that
they were a permanent institution in this country.
What do you suppose would become of a House
of Peers in America?   What has become of the
House of Peers in France?   The name alone remains ;
but where is the power of that brilliant aristocracy
which surrounded the throne of the Louises, and gave
a glitter even to their vices?   Then, what shall we
say of the Church?   I am speaking of it merely from
a secular point of view, as a large and wealthy institution, not exactly of popular origin, nor looked upon
with particular affection by persons who stand well
with the masses.   I call a witness again.   What does
the honourable gentleman the member for Birmingham say?   He speaks of " that portion of the public
" estate which is for a time permitted to remain in the

" hands of the Church of England." What would be
the position of the judges? Looking at the differ-
ences in this respect between the two countries, it
will be seen that we have fenced round our judges
with every safeguard, and given them more and more
power, until we have made them practically an irre-
sponsible class in the country. We have been content to witness the melancholy sight of a person
actually blind, and we still have a man of ninety
years of age sitting upon the judicial bench. We
submit to this, not because we think it right in itself,
but because we think it better to err to a small extent than to give rise to the slightest suspicion that
the position of a judge has been influenced in
the least way by this House. Now, what state of
things exists in America? In the great State of
New York the judges are appointed for six years
only, and farther west the term decreases, until in
Mississippi two years is the *maximum*. And why?
In order that they may be able to administer the law,
not in accordance with the law, but in accordance
with the popular sentiment. That we should continue to have judges I do not doubt, but do you
think they would occupy such a position as they
occupy now, and be so utterly independent of popular
power ?

And now, let us come to ourselves. Our position,
as I have remarked already, is much more honourable
than that of the members of any other Legislative

Assembly in the world. Do you think Democracy would look with a favourable eye upon that? Would it not judge by analogy that such a state of things ought, in some degree, to be altered, and that we should be made to approach nearer to the level of our constituents? Now, we have a privileged class of electors who hold houses above 10*l.* That class is a humble one, but it has discharged its duty up to the present time in a manner which almost defies criticism. But now, without any reason, but merely on account of an abstract principle of right, we have an attempt made to sweep that class away and swamp it in the class below it. Without enlarging upon this topic, I must say it is manifest to me, that if the House of Commons is democratized, it will not rest under such modified circumstances until it has swept away those institutions which at present stand between the people and the Throne, and has supplied the place of them, as far as it can, by institutions deriving their origin directly from the people, being, as the Chancellor of the Duchy of Lancaster said, as representative as possible, and not having the *quasi* independence which the present privileged institutions and corporations possess. You will then have face to face, with no longer anything to break the shock between them, the monarch of the time and a great Democratic Assembly. Now, history has taught us little, if we are to suppose that these two powers would go on harmoniously, and that things

would continue to work as they do now. The event
no one can predict. We saw what a duel there
was in France in 1851, when the President and
the Assembly were each grasping at the sword and
endeavouring to exterminate the other. The Emperor conquered, and Cæsarianism followed. Had
the Emperor failed, France would have had the very
worst possible form of government—namely, a Con-
vention, a deliberative Assembly attempting through
its committees to exercise executive power, and endeavouring to do that which ought to be done
through responsible ministers; and such a Government would only last for a time, to be destroyed
by some Cromwell or Napoleon, or to dissolve by
its own vices and weakness. Look, again, on the
state of things in America, where the President
wields the executive power, and where an opposition
to him is raised in Congress. And then see how
Congress works. It works through committees, and
every officer in the Government has a corresponding
committee in Congress to thwart and to overrule
him. But I need not follow that question farther.
Probably, many gentlemen may even think that I
have endeavoured to look too far into futurity. At
all events, I do not base my case on mere vague conjecture : I base it upon history and experience. The
right honourable gentleman the Chancellor of the
Duchy of Lancaster has told us that England is a
country totally different from America or Australia,

and that no argument could be drawn from either
of the two latter applicable to the position in which
we stand. Well, Sir, there is, of course, no doubt
that England is a country entirely different from
America or Australia, but the difference is in their
favour as regards the working of a Democracy. They
possess boundless tracts of land. In America, land
acts as a sedative to political passion; in England,
it operates as an irritant. Here, land is held up
by democratic leaders to their followers as a thing
to be desired and secured—as the spoils, in fact,
of political warfare; in America, it is, comparatively
speaking, of no value ; it is easily obtained, and much
inflammable matter is in consequence removed, which
would, under other circumstances, prove dangerous to
the system. Everybody knows that if America was
altogether governed by the great towns, the result
would be most disastrous, and that it is the cultivators of the land who moderate their influence, and
prevent them from rushing on to their destruction.
Upon this point I should like to quote the words
of Lord Macaulay, one of the most able of the advo-
cates of the principle of the Reform Bill of 1832,
from which he never went back a hair's-breadth. He,
in replying to an American gentleman who sent him
a " Life of Jefferson," says, speaking of this country:

" In bad years there is plenty of grumbling here,
" and sometimes a little rioting; but it matters little,
" for here the sufferers are not the rulers. The supreme

" power is in the hands of a class, numerous indeed,
" but select—of an educated class—of a class which
" is and knows itself to be deeply interested in the
" security of property and the maintenance of order."

Then he writes as follows :—

" It is quite plain that your Government will never
" be able to restrain a distressed and discontented
" majority, for with you the majority is the Govern-
" ment, and has the rich, who are always a minority,
" absolutely at its mercy. The day will come when,
" in the State of New York, a multitude of people, not
" one of whom has had more than half a breakfast, or
" expects to have more than half a dinner, will choose
" a Legislature."

He adds :—

" Is it possible to doubt what sort of Legislature
" will be chosen ? On one side is a statesman preach-
" ing patience, respect for vested rights, strict obser-
" vance of public faith ; on the other is a demagogue
" ranting about the tyranny of capitalists and usurers,
" and asking why anybody should be permitted to
" drink champagne and to ride in a carriage, while
" thousands of honest folks are in want of necessaries.
" Which of the two candidates is likely to be pre-
" ferred by the working man who hears his children
" crying for more bread ? I seriously apprehend
" that you will in some such season of adversity
" as I have described, do things which will prevent
" prosperity from returning. Either some Caesar or

" Napoleon will seize the reins of government with a
" strong hand, or your Republic will be as fearfully
" plundered and laid waste by barbarians in the
" twentieth century, as the Roman empire was in the
" fifth ; with this difference, that the Huns and Van-
" dals who ravaged the Roman Empire came from
" without, and that your Huns and Vandals will
" have been engendered within your own country and
" by your own institutions."

Now, observe the argument of Lord Macaulay.   It
is this,—" You have a Democracy in America, but
" you have there, also, plenty of elbow-room, and
" abundant means of subsistence for its whole popula-
" tion ; but when this state of things comes to an end,
" then the institutions of the country will be tried,
" and a crash may follow."   In England we have not
a Democracy, but we have a state of society in which,
in the event of pressure, distress and misery must to a
great extent prevail.   Now, if we add here, with our
hands, Democracy to population, as the course of time
may in America add population to Democracy, we
shall have done all in our power to bring about
exactly the state of things which Lord Macaulay describes, and we may expect that something like the
same consequences will be the result.

Sir, it appears to me we have more and more
reason, every day we live, to regret the loss of Lord
Palmerston.   The remaining members of his Government would seem, by way of a mortuary contribution,

to have buried in his grave all their prudence, statesmanship, and moderation. He was scarcely withdrawn from the scene before they set to work to con-
travene and contradict his policy. That policy, acted
upon by a statesman who perfectly understood the
wants of the English people, had been crowned with
unexampled success, and they, I suppose, must have
thought that the best way to secure a continuance of
that success was to aim at doing that which he above
all other things disapproved. The noble lord at the
head of the Government, and the right honourable
gentleman the Chancellor of the Exchequer, have
performed a great feat : they have taken the great
mass of their supporters, who are, I believe, men of
moderate views and moderate opinions, and laid them
at the feet of the honourable member for Birmingham. They have thus brought them into contact
with men and with principles from which but six
short months ago they would have recoiled. That is
what has happened to a portion of those who sit upon
these benches. As to the rest of us, we are left like
sheep in the wilderness, and after the success of thi
extraordinary combination—to use no harsher word—
we who remain precisely what we have been are
charged with inconsistency, while the bonds of political allegiance are being strained until they are ready
to crack for the purpose of keeping the Liberal party
together. We are told that we are bound by every
tie which ought to bind mankind, to act in accordance

with the policy of Earl Russell; but I, for one, Sir, dispute the justice of that proposition. I have never served under that noble lord. I have served under two prime ministers for a period—I am sorry to say —of little less than ten years. The one was Lord Aberdeen, the other Lord Palmerston. Earl Russell joined the Government of each of those Ministers; both Governments he abandoned, both he assisted to destroy. I owe the noble lord no allegiance. I am not afraid of the people of this country. They have displayed a good sense which is remarkable indeed, when contrasted with the harangues which have been addressed to them. But if I am not afraid of the people, neither do I agree with the right honourable gentleman the member for Huntingdon, in fearing those by whom they are led. Demagogues are the commonplace of history. They are to be found wherever popular commotion has prevailed, and they all bear to one another a strong family likeness. Their names float lightly on the stream of time; they are in some way handed down to us, but then they are as little regarded as is the foam which rides on the crest of the stormy wave and bespatters the rock which it cannot shake. Such men, Sir, I do not fear; but I have, I confess, some misgivings when I see a number of gentlemen of rank, of character, of property, and intelligence, carried away without being convinced, or even over-persuaded, in the support of a policy which many of them in their inmost hearts detest and abhor. Monarchies exist by loyalty, aristocracies by honour, popular assemblies by political virtue and patriotism, and it is in the loss of those things, and not in comets and eclipses, that we are to look for the portents that herald the fall of States.

I have said that I am utterly unable to reason with the Chancellor of the Exchequer for want of a common principle to start from ; but there is happily one common ground left to us, and that is the second book of the Æneid of Virgil. My right honourable friend, like the moth which has singed its wings in the candle, has returned again to the poor old Trojan horse, and I shall, with the permission of the House, give them one more excerpt from the history of that noble beast, first premising that I shall then turn him out to grass, at all events for the remainder of the Session. The passage which I am about to quote is one which is, I think, worthy the attention of the House, because it contains a description not only of the invading army of which we have heard so much, but also a slight sketch of its general :—

> " Arduus armatos mediis in mœnibus adstans
> Fundit equus, victorque Sinon incendia miscet
> Insultans; portis alii bipatentibus adsunt,
> Millia quot magnis nunquam venêre Mycenis."

In other words :—

> " The fatal horse pours forth the human tide,
> Insulting Sinon flings his firebrands wide,
> The gates are burst; the ancient rampart falls,
> And swarming millions climb its crumbling walls."

I have now, Sir, traced as well as I can what I believe
will be the natural results of a measure which, it
seems to my poor imagination, is calculated, if it
should pass into law, to destroy one after another
those institutions which have secured for England an
amount of happiness and prosperity which no country
has ever reached, or is ever likely to attain.   Surely
the heroic work of so many centuries, the matchless
achievements of so many wise heads and strong hands,
deserve a nobler consummation than to be sacrificed
at the shrine of revolutionary passion, or the maudlin
enthusiasm of humanity?   But, if we do fall, we shall
fall deservedly.   Uncoerced by any external force,
not borne down by any internal calamity, but in the
full plethora of our wealth and the surfeit of our too
exuberant prosperity, with our own rash and inconsiderate hands, we are about to pluck down on our
own heads the venerable temple of our liberty and
our glory.   History may tell of other acts as signally
disastrous, but of none more wanton, none more
disgraceful.

SPEECH ON THE REPRESENTATION OF THE PEOPLE BILL, AND THE REDISTRIBUTION OF SEATS BILL.

May 31, 1866.

Mr. Speaker, we are now called upon to go into committee on a Bill which has never been read a second time. The two halves of it have been read, each of them a second time, but the whole measure we have never until this moment had before us. The first half this House was induced—or shall I say coerced?—into reading a second time without knowledge of the other part. The second half was really hurried on so fast to a second reading—only an interval of a week being given to master all its complicated details—that I, for one, was quite unable to take part in the discussion on the second reading, for want of time to make up my mind as to an opinion by which I should be willing to stand. I hope, therefore, the House will allow me, even at this stage, to question the principle of the measure. What is that principle? I must apologize to the House for the monotonous nature of my complaints, which are, I think, justified by the uniform nature of the provocation I receive. That provocation is that the Government keeps continually bringing in measures, attacking, as it seems to me, the very vital and fundamental institutions of the country, and purposely abstains from telling us the principle of those measures. I made the same complaint, I am sorry to say, against the Chancellor of the Exchequer on the Franchise Bill. I make it again now. The Chancellor of the Exchequer, in introducing the Redistribution Bill, said that the Government was not desirous of innovation— that is to say, they went upon no principle. Their principle, he said, was the same as the principle of every Redistribution Bill. Now, that appears to me to be impossible, because Redistribution Bills may be divided into two classes. There is one, the great Reform Bill—the only successful Redistribution Bill that anyone ever heard of, and then there are the four which succeeded it, and which all failed from one cause or another. The principle of the Reform Bill was one thing, and the principle of the four Bills which followed it was another. The principle of the Reform Bill was, no doubt, disfranchisement. The feeling of the country at that time was, that the deliberations of this House were overruled, and the public opinion of the country stifled, by an enormous number of small boroughs under the patronage of noblemen and persons of property. That state of

things was considered a public nuisance, and one
which it was desirable to abate, and hence the principle of the Reform Bill was disfranchisement, and
141 members were taken away from the small boroughs. The Government proposition was to reduce
the number of the House of Commons by fifty, because
they were very anxious to get rid of these members, and
they had no means which appeared suitable of filling
up the vacancies they had created. It was only on an
amendment carried against the Government that it
was determined not to diminish the number of members in this House. But has that been the principle
of any subsequent Reform Bill? I think not; it has
been quite the contrary. It has been the principle of
enfranchisement; and of disfranchisement only so far
as may be necessary in order to fill up the places
which require enfranchisement. As I have shown the
House, there are two different principles, and the
right honourable gentleman does not tell me which
is his, but says the principle is that of all other Redistribution Bills. This puts me in mind of the story
of a lady who wrote to a friend to ask how she was to
receive a particular lover, and the answer was, " As
" you receive all your other lovers." Well, as the
Chancellor of the Exchequer will not tell us what the
principle of his measure is, I must, I am sorry to say,
with the same monotony of treatment, try to puzzle
it out for myself, for it seems to me preposterous to
consider the Bill without the guiding thought of those

who constructed it.   There is one principle of re-distribution upon which it clearly ought not to be founded, and that is the principle of abstract right to equality of representation.   The principle of equal electoral districts, or an approximation to such districts, is not the principle upon which a Redistribution Bill ought to be based.   To adopt such a principle would be to make us the slaves of numbers—very good servants, but very bad masters.   I do not suppose we are generally eager to see the time—

> " When each fair burgh, numerically free,
>   Returns its Members by the Rule of Three."

And yet, though few persons stand up for the principle of equality of representation, I cannot escape the conclusion that it has had a good deal to do with the matter, and that the Government will find it exceedingly difficult to point out what other principle than that of a sort of approximation towards numerical equality has guided them.   For if it be not a principle of *à priori* rights, it must be some good to the State, some improvement of the House or the Government —some practical good in some way.   Now, the House has had the advantage of hearing the Chancellor of the Exchequer, the Secretary of State for the Colonies, and the Chancellor of the Duchy of Lancaster, and I ask whether any of these right honourable gentlemen has pointed out any good of any practical nature whatever to be expected from the Bill.   I set myself, therefore, according to my old method, to try and puzzle out what ought to be the principle of a Bill for the Redistribution of Seats. In the first place, I should like to be shown some practical evil to be remedied, but I give that up in despair, for I have so often asked for it and failed to obtain it, that I am quite sure I shall not have it on this occasion. But it seems to me a reasonable view of a Redistribution Bill, that it should make this House, more fully and perfectly than it is at present, a reflection of the opinion of the country. That, I think, is a fair ground to start from. We have suffered in many respects from the arbitrary division of these two measures, and in none more than this—that the arguments for the Redistribution of Seats have been transferred to this Bill for enlarging the franchise. For, although it is quite true that a Bill for the Redistribution of Seats should aim at making Parliament a mirror of the country, it is also true that there can be nothing more inappropriate than the argument when applied to the enlargement of the franchise. For to pass a Bill which puts the power in a majority of the boroughs into the hands of the working classes, is not to make this House a faithful reflection of the opinion of the country, but is to make it an inversion of that opinion by giving political power into the hands of those who have very little social power of any kind. But that principle applies, to a certain extent, to a Redistribution Bill, and from that point I take my departure. Any one who makes an examination as to

the nature of the deficiency, will see whether this
House fails in any considerable degree to reflect the
opinion of the country. I confess I have found it exceedingly difficult to discover in what respects it fails
to do so. I have, indeed, observed some tendency of
a kind, which, if we are to have a Redistribution Bill,
ought to be corrected. I think there is a visible
tendency to too great a uniformity and monotony of
representation. I think there is a danger that we
may become too much like each other—that we may
become merely the multiple of one number. That is
a danger which has occurred to thinking men, and I
think it is very desirable that in a Redistribution Bill
we should find a remedy, if possible, for the tendency
to this level of monotony, and perhaps mediocrity. I
think another great object we must have in view in a
Redistribution Bill should be enfranchisement, and by
that I mean not the aggregation of fresh members to
large constituencies, but the enfranchisement of fresh
constituencies, and by the enfranchisement of such
constituencies the giving more variety and life to the
representation of the country, and thus making the
House what the country is — a collection of infinite
variety of all sorts of pursuits and habits. I think the
second advantage is, that by making fresh constituencies
by fresh enfranchisements, you do the most efficient
thing you can do towards moderating the frightful,
enormous, and increasing expenses of elections. This .
is one of the greatest evils of our present system. I am

not speaking of the illegitimate expenses of elections,
but of the legitimate expenses. We had a paper laid
upon our tables this morning giving an account of the
expenses of elections from " S " downwards. I take the
first few large boroughs, and I will read the expenses.
The expense of the election for Stafford is 5400*l*.;
Stoke-upon-Trent, 6200*l*.; Sunderland, 5000*l*.; and
Westminster, 12,000*l*. These are the aggregate expenses of all the candidates. I take them as they
come, without picking and choosing. I wish to call
particular attention to the case of Westminster, not
for the purpose of saying anything disagreeable to
my honourable friend (Mr. J. Stuart Mill), for we
know he was elected in a burst—I will say a well-
directed burst—of popular enthusiasm. That was
honourable to him and honourable to them, and I
have no doubt that in the course of the election all
that could be done by industry and enthusiasm was
accomplished—gratuitously; and I am sure that my
honourable friend did not contribute in any way to
swell any unreasonable election expenses. His election ought to have been gratuitous; but mark what
it cost—2302*l*. I believe it did not cost him 6*d*.
He refused to contribute anything, and it was very
much to the honour of his constituents that they
brought him in gratuitously. But look to the state
of our election practices, when such an outburst of
popular feeling could not be given effect to without
that enormou sacrifice of money. I will now call

attention to two or three counties. This subject has
not been sufficiently dwelt upon, but it bears materially
upon the question before us to-night. I will take the
southern division of Derbyshire. The election cost
8500*l.*, and this is the cheapest I shall read. The
northern division of Durham cost 14,620*l.*, and the
southern division 11,000*l.* South Essex cost 10,000*l.*;
West Kent cost 12,000*l.*; South Lancashire, 17,000*l.*;
South Shropshire, 12,000*l.*; North Staffordshire,
14,000*l.*; North Warwickshire, 10,000*l.*; South Warwickshire, 13,000*l.*; North Wiltshire, 13,000*l.*; South
Wiltshire, 12,000*l.* ; and the North Riding of Yorkshire, 27,000*l.*—all legitimate expenses, but by no
means the whole expense. Now, I ask the House
how it is possible that the institutions of this country
can endure, if this kind of thing is to go on and
increase. Do not suppose for a moment that this is
favourable to anything aristocratic. It is quite the
contrary. It is favourable to a plutocracy working
upon a democracy. Think of the persons excluded
by such a system! You want rank, wealth, good
connections, and gentleman-like demeanour, but you
also want sterling talent and ability for the business
of the country, and how can you expect it when no
man can stand who is not prepared to pay a considerable proportion of such frightful expenses? I think
I am not wrong in saying that another object of the
Redistribution Bill might very well be to diminish
the expense of elections by diminishing the size

of the electoral districts. These are the objects
which I picture to myself ought to be aimed at by
a Redistribution Bill. It should aim at variety and
economy, and should look upon disfranchisement as
a means of enfranchisement. And now, having done
with that, I will just approach the Bill, and having
trespassed inordinately on former occasions upon the
time of the House, I will now only allude to two
points. One is the grouping and the other is adding
the third member to counties and boroughs. This
word "group" is very pretty and picturesque. It reminds one of Watteau and Wouvermans—of a group
of young ladies, of pretty children, of tulips, or anything else of that kind. But it really is a word of
most disagreeable significance when analyzed, because
it means disfranchising a borough, and in a very
uncomfortable manner refranchising it. It means
disfranchising the integer, and refranchising and
replacing it by exceedingly vulgar fractions. Well,
now, I ask myself why do we disfranchise and why do
we enfranchise? I do not speak now of the eight
members got by taking the second member from
boroughs, but of the forty-one got by grouping—
by disfranchisement and enfranchisement. And I
ask, in the first place, why disfranchise these small
boroughs? I have heard no answer to this from the
Government. All that was attempted was said by
the Chancellor of the Exchequer—that he had in
1859 advocated the maintenance of small boroughs

on the ground that they admitted young men of
talent to that House, but he found on examination
that they did not admit young men of talent; and,
therefore, he ceased to advocate the retention of small
boroughs.   My right honourable friend is possibly
satisfied with his own reasoning.   He answered his
own argument to his own satisfaction; but what I
wanted to hear is, not only that the argument he used
seven years ago had ceased to have any influence on
his own mind, but what the argument is which has
induced the Government to disfranchise the boroughs.
Of this, he said not a single syllable.   I know my
own position too well to offer anything in favour of
small boroughs.   That would not come with a good
grace from me ; but I have a duty to perform to some
of my constituents.   They are not all ambitious of
the honours of martyrdom.   So I will give a very
good argument in favour of small boroughs.   What is
the character of the House of Commons ?—

"It is a character of extreme diversity of repre-
"sentation.   Elections by great bodies, agricultural,
"commercial, or manufacturing, in our counties and
"great cities, are balanced by the right of election
"in boroughs of small or moderate population, which
"are thus admitted to fill up the defects and complete
"the fulness of our representation."
I need not say that I am reading from the work of
a Prime Minister.   Not only that, but he re-published
it in the spring of last year, and in that edition this

passage is not there. But he published a second and more popular edition in the autumn, and in the autumn of last year he inserted the passage I am now reading. The Prime Minister differs from the Chancellor of the Duchy, for he seems fonder of illustration than argument—

" For instance, Mr. Thomas Baring " (he goes on to say), " from his commercial eminence, from his high "character, from his world-wide position, ought to "be a member of the House of Commons. His "political opinions, and nothing but his political "opinions, prevent his being the fittest person to be "a member for the city of London."
It would be better to have said, "his political opinions " prevent his being a member for the city of London," without saying they prevent his being "the fittest " person," which is invidious—

" But the borough of Huntingdon, with 2654 in- " habitants and 393 registered voters, elects him " willingly." Next he instances my right hon. friend the Secretary of State for the Home Department; but, as he happily stands aside and looks upon the troubles of the small boroughs as the gods of Lucretius did upon the troubles of mankind, I will not read all the pretty things which the Prime Minister says of him. Then we come next to the Attorney-General—

" Sir Roundell Palmer is, *omnium consensu*, well " qualified to enlighten the House of Commons on " any question of municipal or international law, and

"to expound the true theory and practice of law
"reform.   He could not stand for Westminster or
"Middlesex, for Lancashire or Yorkshire, with much
"chance of success."

The House will observe that that was written last
autumn.   If it had been written this morning, I
think very possibly the Prime Minister might have
cancelled these words, and said, "The honourable
"and learned gentleman would have stood for one of
"those large constituencies with every prospect of
"success."   Now, is it credible, is it possible to conceive, that the writer of these words should actually
be the Premier of the Government which, not six
months after these illustrations were given, has
introduced this new Reform Bill to group and
disfranchise the very boroughs he thus instanced?
Well, there is a little more—

"Dr. Temple says, in a letter to the *Daily News*,
"'I know that when Emerson was in England he
"'regretted to me that all the more cultivated classes
"'in America abstained *from politics, because they felt*
"'*themselves hopelessly swamped.*'"

These last words are given in italics, the only construction I can put upon which is, that the noble
lord thought, if many of these small boroughs were
disfranchised, the persons he desires to see in this
House would not come here, else I do not see what
is the application of the passage.   He goes on to say—

"It is very rare to find a man of literary taste and

"cultivated understanding expose himself to the rough
"reception of the election of a large city."
There is a compliment here to many of the noble
lord's most ardent supporters. But he continues—

"The small boroughs, by returning men of know-
"ledge acquired in the study, and of temper mode-
"rated in the intercourse of refined society"—
Where the members for large boroughs never go, I
suppose—

"Restore the balance which Marylebone and Man-
"chester, if left even with the 10*l.* franchise undis-
"puted masters of the field, would radically disturb."
Whether that means to disturb from the roots or to
disturb from radicalism, I do not know—

"But, besides this advantage, they act with the
"counties in giving that due influence to property
"without which our House of Commons would very
"inadequately represent the nation, and thus make
"it feasible to admit the householders of our large
"towns to an extent which would otherwise be in-
"equitable, and possibly lead to injurious results."
So that the proposal of the noble lord's Government,
coupled as it is with the disfranchisement of these small
boroughs, is in his opinion inequitable certainly, and
possibly likely to lead to injurious results. He goes on—

"These are the reasons why, in my opinion, after
"abolishing 141 seats by the Reform Act, it is not
"expedient that the smaller boroughs should be
"extinguished by any further large process of dis-

" franchisement. The last Reform Bill of Lord
" Palmerston's Government went quite far enough
" in this direction."

Now, Sir, what did the last Reform Bill of Lord
Palmerston do? It took away the second member
from twenty-five boroughs, and that was the whole
of it. It did not break up a single electoral district.
The present Bill takes away forty-nine members from
these places, and, therefore, according to the words of
the Prime Minister, written six months ago, it exactly
doubles what the Ministry ought to do in the matter.
After that, I think the House will agree with me that
it would not become the member for Calne to add
anything in defence of his borough; for what could
he say that the Prime Minister had not said a
hundred times better, and with all the authority
and weight of such a statesman, writing deliberately
in his study no less than thirty-three years after the
passing of the Reform Act? Well, I shall say no
more of that; but, for some reason which we have yet
to hear, I will assume that the small boroughs are to
be disfranchised. The next question that we have to
consider is, what is to be done with the seats to be
acquired by that disfranchisement. It does seem to
me quite absurd to halt between two opinions in this
way. I must assume that there is some good and
cogent reason for disfranchising the small boroughs,
or else, I suppose, they would let us alone. But if
there be a good and cogent reason for disfranchising

them, what possible reason can there be for re-
enfranchising them immediately afterwards? What
reason can there be for giving them back as a frac-
tion that which you have taken away as an integer?
The first process condemns the second. It may be
right and wise—I do not in my conscience think it is
—to disfranchise these boroughs; but if you do take
that course, your business surely should be to do the
best you can for the interests of the country at large
with the seats you thus obtain. If you are to be
influenced by respect for traditions and by veneration
for antiquity, perhaps Calne should have some claim,
because it was there that the memorable encounter is
said to have taken place between St. Dunstan and
his enemies, which terminated in the combatants all
tumbling through the floor, with the exception of the
saint himself. And I may remind you that in our
own times Calne was represented by Dunning, by
Lord Henry Petty, by Mr. Abercromby, for some
time Speaker of this House, and by Lord Macaulay.
That might avail something; but if it is all to go
for nothing, I ask on what principle, having first
broken up the electoral system of these boroughs
and taken away their franchise, you begin to reconstruct them into these groups? If you are actuated
by a veneration for antiquity, or by an indisposition
to destroy a state of things which is, if not carried too
far, in no slight degree advantageous, and cases very
much the working of the Government of the country,

besides introducing into this House a class of persons, some of whom you would do very badly without—if that be so, leave these boroughs alone. If it be not, deal with the question in a bold and manly spirit; but do not take a thing away from them because you say it is wrong they should have it, and then give it them back again in part, because you say it is right they should have it. That involves a contradiction. Look at what you are doing. You take away the franchise from these places, and then you limit yourself by giving it to boroughs which have previously possessed it. You unite together boroughs that have been in the habit of engrossing for themselves all the care and attention of a single member, who is obliged to pay great regard to their wishes, to look after their little wants, to pet them, and coddle them, and make much of them. That which he has been used to do for one of these boroughs he will still be expected to do, and must do, after they are grouped; and what he does and pays for one of the group he will have to do and pay for all the rest. Not one of the three or four will bate one jot or tittle of its claim upon the member or candidate, but everything will be multiplied by so many times as there are separate places in the group. You must have as many agents in each of them, you must give as many subscriptions to their charities, their schools, and their volunteers. Everything of that kind, in fact, will be multiplied

by this system three or four fold. Now, these
boroughs at present give you a great advantage.
All must admit that there is an advantage, if it is
not bought too dear, in having means by which
persons who are not of large fortune can obtain seats
in this House. But by this Bill you take away that
one clear advantage of these boroughs, the one thing
for which, I think, they very worthily exist—you
make them very expensive constituencies, and you
then retain them, out of veneration for antiquity and
from a traditionary feeling, when you have stripped
them of the very merit which recommends them to
the friends of the Constitution! Well, Sir, it is polygamy for a man to marry three or four wives; but
that comparison does not do justice to this particular
case, because you enforce an aggravated form of
political polygamy by asking a man to marry three
or four widows. The House need not be afraid of
my pursuing that branch of the subject. The best
that can be said for the Ministerial Bill—at least,
what has been said for it—is, that it is intended to
remove anomalies. I really know of no other defence
that is offered for it than that. Well, Sir, mankind
will tolerate many anomalies if they are old, and if,
as they have grown up, they have got used to them.
They will also tolerate anomalies if they have been
necessarily occasioned by the desire to work out
improvements. But when people set about correcting anomalies, and so do their work as to leave

behind them and to create even worse anomalies than any they found existing, neither gods nor men can stand it. Is not that the case here? I would briefly call attention to two or three of the proposed groups. In Cornwall, you have Bodmin, Liskeard, and Launceston, with 18,000 inhabitants between them, thrown into a group; but the towns of Redruth, Penzance, and others, making up altogether 23,000, in the same county, are left without the means of representation. Then, in the county of Devon, you are to have Totnes joined with Dartmouth and Ashburton, and, by putting the three places together, you only get 11,500 people; but there is Torquay, with 16,000, that you leave entirely unrepresented. I should not object to that, because, if a thing works well, you do not do wrong in leaving it alone; but if you do begin to meddle with it, it is monstrous to turn everything upside down, and then introduce a thousand times greater anomalies than those you have removed. People will bear with anomalies that are old, historical, and familiar, and that, after all, answer some useful end; but they revolt at them when you show them how flagrant an injustice and inequality the House of Commons or the Government will perpetrate in the name of equality and justice. Then there is the group of Maldon and Harwich, thirty miles apart. The Chancellor of the Duchy of Lancaster was much shocked at our objecting to these boroughs being

joined in this extraordinary way; but, Sir, were we
not told by the Chancellor of the Exchequer that
these things were done upon geographical considerations? The geographical considerations referred to
by the Chancellor of the Exchequer appear to me
to mean, as interpreted by his Bill, that the members
for the towns to be grouped should learn as much
geography as possible by having as large distances as
possible to travel over. Then we have Gloucester-
shire and Worcestershire, Cirencester, Tewkesbury,
and Evesham, with 16,000 inhabitants; but in
Worcestershire alone you have Oldbury and Stour-
bridge, with a population of 23,000, which remain
utterly unrepresented. Again, there is the case of
Wells and Westbury, which scrape together 11,000
inhabitants, while between the two we find Yeovil
with 8000, and for which nothing is done. In
Wiltshire, Chippenham, Malmesbury, and Calne,
have 19,000 inhabitants, but a very few miles from
Calne is Trowbridge, with 9626 inhabitants, the
second town in the county, which you leave unrepresented. In Yorkshire, Richmond and Northal-
lerton scrape together 9000 inhabitants, while for
Barnsley, with 17,000, Doncaster, 16,000, and
Keighley, 15,000, you do nothing at all. Such
things may be tolerable when they have grown up
with you, but they are utterly intolerable when a
Government interferes, and introduces a measure
which overlooks such cases while professing to take

numbers as its guide. The Government have repudiated geographical considerations, but it is more
absurd if taken numerically. Here is, however, something worse than an anomaly : it is a gross injustice. The House is aware—with the two exceptions
of Bewdley and Droitwich, which are probably to
be accounted for by haste and carelessness, the
matter being a small one—that all the boroughs
having a less population than 8000 inhabitants are
dealt with in some way or other. There are two ways
of treating these boroughs. There is a gentler and
there is a severer form. There are eight boroughs which
are picked out for what I will call the question ordinary—that is, losing one member, and the remainder,
a very large number, are picked out and formed into
sixteen groups, this being the extraordinary or exquisite
torture, being pounded to pieces, brayed in a mortar,
and then renovated. In judging of the treatment
which these boroughs receive, I think some principle
ought to be observed. The geographical principle
has been ostentatiously set aside, and look at what
has happened to the numerical principle. There
is Newport, in the Isle of Wight, with 8000 inhabitants, which loses only one of its members, and is not
grouped ; while Bridport, with 7819 inhabitants,
loses both its members and is grouped. There are
seven boroughs having smaller populations than
Bridport, from which only one member is taken,
and they are not grouped ; while Bridport, with

a larger population, has both its members taken,
and is grouped. Is it on account of geographical
considerations that it is coupled with Honiton, nineteen miles off? [An honourable Member: Twenty-
one!] That is not an anomaly: it is simply a gross
injustice. There is Chippenham, with 7075 inhabitants. Chippenham, as every one knows, is a
rising railway town. Yet it is grouped; while there
are five boroughs which contain fewer inhabitants
than Chippenham, which will each continue to return
one member. Going a little farther, we find Dorchester with 6779 inhabitants, and three boroughs
smaller than itself. Dorchester loses both members,
while the three boroughs smaller than Dorchester,
retain one member: they are Hertford, Great Mar-
low, and Huntingdon. I can simply attribute the
cause of this to the great haste, carelessness, and in-
advertency which have characterized this measure. I
am far from attributing it to any improper motives.
I have not the slightest notion of anything of the
kind. It arises, I believe, from the mere wantonness
or carelessness of the Government hurrying forward a
Bill which they did not intend to bring in. and which
they were at last compelled to bring in, contrary to
all their declarations. Between Huntingdon, the
smallest borough that loses one member, and Newport, the largest, there are seventeen boroughs, nine
of them returning one member each, and eight returning two, all of which have larger populations

than Huntingdon, which is allowed to retain one member, while they are grouped. The reason I cannot tell; but there stands the anomaly. This grouping of boroughs cannot, therefore, I say, be satisfactory to any class of gentlemen. Of course it is not satisfactory to the small boroughs. They are the material out of which other people are to be compensated, and of course no one likes to be included in such a process. But I cannot imagine that it can be satisfactory to gentlemen who call for those measures with a view to remove anomalies and promote equality, and make the Parliament a more accurate representative of the population of the country. It seems to me, that everybody must be dissatisfied with such a proceeding as this. The House need not take all these groups as they stand, because any one of them might be remedied in committee; but the whole principle of the thing is so bad that it is absolutely impossible to deal with it in committee at all. I have been assuming, hitherto, that we have good grounds for getting these forty-nine members that are wanted, but that depends entirely upon the use the Government make of them when they have them. What do they do with them? They propose to give out of these forty-nine, twenty-five as third members to counties, and four as third members to large towns, and seven to Scotland. I deny that a case is made out in favour of this arrangement. Honourable gentlemen opposite, with whom I sympathise so much on this question, may not, perhaps, agree with me on this point. I maintain that it is a mere illusion, as things now stand, and looking at these two measures as a whole, to talk of county representation; you must look at the two things together, franchise and redistribution, and you must remember that the counties you give these members to are to become really groups of towns. Every one knows very well where the houses between 14*l.* and 50*l.* are to be found. They are to be found, not in the rural districts, but in the towns. What you are preparing to do for the county members is to make a total change in the nature of their constituency. But under the system proposed, the county member would no longer represent a constituency which from its present and peculiar character can easily be worked as a whole. When you lower the franchise as proposed, you have taken the power out of the rural districts and given it to the small towns. The member will therefore have to reckon with so many small towns, with probably an attorney in each. When you speak of giving a third member to counties, you must remember that you are talking of counties not as they are now, but as you propose to make them. It is an illusion, therefore, to say that a great deal is done for the rural districts in thus adding members to the counties, and this will be the more easily understood if you have not forgotten the opinion of Lord Russell, who says how materially the

small boroughs assist the counties in maintaining the
balance of power. I altogether decline to be caught
by that bait. But, putting that aside, on what principle are we to give three members to counties?
It has been the practice to give two members to
counties from time immemorial, with a slight exception at the time of the Reform, which is by no
means generally approved. I am willing to accept
the fact without stopping to inquire too curiously
whether this number was fixed upon because they
slept in the same bed or rode on the same horse
on their journeys to London. But, if you come to
make it a general practice to give three members
to counties, I think we are entitled to ask upon what
principle this is to be done. For my own part, I can
suggest no other principle than the mere worship of
numbers. It is quite a new principle that numbers
should not only be represented in this House because
they are important, but that that importance should
entitle them to more votes. The House will recollect
that every member has two separate and distinct
duties to perform. He is the representative of the
borough which sends him to Parliament, and he has
to look after its local interests to the best of his
power. That is a small and, in the mild and just
times in which we live, generally a comparatively
easy duty; but his greater and more pre-eminent
duty is to look after the affairs of the empire. The
real use, therefore, of an electoral district, be it small

or large, is one more important than the adequate representation of the numbers of any particular place,
so long as they are represented. It is, that it should
send to Parliament the persons best calculated to
make laws, and perform the other functions demanded
of the members of this House. This seems to me to
go directly against the principle that these great com-
munities are not only entitled to send competent
gentlemen to represent their affairs, but to send as
many members as will correspond with their weight
in the country. If once you grant this principle, you
are advancing far on the road to electoral districts
and numerical equality. I say this is the mere principle of numbers. If the principle be once established,
it is very easy to give it extension. Scarcely a meeting is assembled on this subject, without some man
getting up and complaining that the member for
a small borough, myself, for instance, should have
a vote which will counterbalance the vote of the
representative of a borough containing 200,000 or
300,000. If it was a fight for the good things of this
world between Calne and Birmingham, I could understand how such a principle might be adopted ; but
when it is a question of making the laws and in-
fluencing the destinies of this country, the question is,
not which is the larger body, but which best dis-
charges its duty in sending members to Parliament.
I cannot find a trace of that principle in the whole of
this Bill, for it is clear that there is no such idea

in giving these three members to counties.   They are
mere concessions to the importance of the constituencies to which they are given, while the small boroughs
are grouped in a manner likely to promote mediocrity, because gentlemen of shining qualities and useful attainments will scarcely be able to contest them,
unless possessed of great wealth.   I cannot bring my
mind to the idea of giving three members to those
large constituencies.   We should, on the whole, be
far better without those twenty-nine members.   We
had better leave matters alone, if we can find no
better use for them.   Now, I have gone through
what I have to say upon the details of this Bill; and
perhaps the House will allow me to sum up what
I think of the whole effect of the Ministerial measure.   You say how frightful the expenses of elections
are, and declare that they are a cankerworm in
the very heart of the Constitution.   Yet what is the
effect of this Bill with regard to the legitimate expenses of elections?   The Government are proposing
to increase the size of the constituency of every
borough in the kingdom.   Will that decrease expense? They propose to disfranchise small boroughs;
and, instead of subdividing districts with a view
to make more manageable constituencies, except in
the case of the Tower Hamlets and South Lancashire, a senseless homage is paid to mere numbers,
adding to that which is already too much.   Then
there is another thing.   It is the duty of every man

who calls himself a statesman, to study the signs
of the times, and make himself master, as far as
he can. of the tendencies of society. What are those
signs and tendencies? I suppose we shall none of us
doubt that they are tending more or less in the direction, as I said before, of uniformity and democracy.
What, then, is the duty of a wise statesman under
such circumstances? Is it to stimulate the tendencies which are already in full force and activity
or is it not rather, if he cannot leave matters alone, to
see if he cannot find some palliative? If he cannot
prevent the change which stronger powers are working, should he not make that change as smooth as
possible, and not by any means accelerate it? But
the whole of this Bill is not in the way of moderating, but stimulating, existing tendencies. It is not
always wise (and the observation is as old as Aristotle)
to make a law too accurately in correspondence with
the times, or the genius of the Government under
which you live. The best law that could be made for
the United States would not be one peculiarly democratic. The best law for the French Government
to enact is not one of an ultra-monarchical character.
There is sound wisdom in this, and it should be kept well
in mind; but it seems to have been by no means considered by the framers of the crude measure before us.

> " But our new John spurs the hot-mouth'd horse,
>   Instructs him well to know his native force,
>   To take the bit between his teeth, and fly
>   To the next headlong steep of anarchy."

Passing to another point, I have to remind you that
the Chancellor of the Exchequer frightened us the
other day by giving us a prose version of Byron's
poem on " Darkness," when we were told that our
coal was all going to be consumed, and then we were
to die like the last man and woman of our mutual
hideousness. Upon that the right honourable gentleman founded a proposition, and never was so practical a proposition worked out upon so speculative a
basis. You will have no coal in 100 years, he says,
and therefore pay your debts ; and, addressing honourable gentlemen opposite, he says, " Commerce
" may die, navigation may die, and manufactures
" may die—and die they will —but land will remain,
" and you will be saddled with the debt." That was
the language of the right honourable gentleman.
Now, if we are to pay terminable annuities on the
strength of the loss of our coal, do not you think we
may well apply the same dogma to this proposed
Reform of our Constitution ? What is the right
honourable gentleman seeking to do by this Bill ?
He is seeking to take away power of control from the
land—from that which is to remain when all those
fine things I have mentioned have passed away in
the future—from that which will be eventually saddled with the whole burden of the debt, and to place
it in these fugitive and transitory elements which,
according to the account he gave us, a breath has
made and a breath can unmake. I ask, is that, upon

the right honourable gentleman's own showing, sound prospective wisdom ? I do not deal myself with such remote contingencies ; I offer this simply as an *argumentum ad hominem.* I should like to hear the answer. I have a word to say with regard to the franchise. We have had a little light let in upon this subject. We are offered, as you all know, a 7*l.* franchise. It is defended by the Chancellor of the Exchequer upon two grounds—flesh and blood, and fathers of families. The 7*l.* franchise is defended by the honourable member for Birmingham upon another ground ; he takes his stand on the ancient lines of the British Constitution. I will suggest to him one line of the British Constitution, and I should like to know whether he means to stand by it. In his campaign of 1858, in which he had taken some liberties with the Crown, and spoke with some disrespect of the temporal peers, he came to the spiritual peers, and this was the language he employed. He said, " That creature of monstrous—nay, of adulterous " birth." I suppose there is no part of the British Constitution much more ancient than the spiritual peers. Is that one of the lines the honourable gentleman takes his stand upon ? Again, the Attorney-General, having recovered from the blow the grouping of Richmond must have been to him, has become a convert, and, like most converts, he is an enthusiast. He tells us that he is for the 7*l.* franchise because he is in favour, like the honourable member for Birmingham, of household suffrage. These are the reasons which are given in order to induce us to adopt the 7*l.* franchise. I ask the House, is there any encouragement in any of these arguments to adopt it? The Chancellor of the Exchequer says it is flesh and blood; it is a very small instalment of flesh and blood, and none can doubt that any one asking for it upon that ground only asks for it as a means to get more flesh and blood. The honourable member for Birmingham stands upon the Constitution, and he puts me in mind of the American squib, which says—

> "Here we stand on the Constitution, by thunder,
> It's a fact of which there are bushels of proofs,
> For how could we trample upon it, I wonder,
> If it wasn't continually under our hoofs!"

Well, the honourable gentleman asks the 7*l.* upon the ground that it is constitutional—that is, upon the ground of household suffrage. He wants it with a view of letting us down gently to household suffrage. The Attorney-General, of course, means the same. In fact, he said we ought to do it at once. But see what a condemnation the Attorney-General passes upon the Government of which he forms a part. He says, "You have taken your stand upon the " 7*l.* franchise. The ground you take is so slippery " and unsafe, so utterly untenable, that I would " rather go down to household suffrage at once—to " the veriest cabin with a door and a chimney to it " that can be called a house. There I may, perhaps,

" touch ground." What encouragement do these
gentlemen give us to take the 7l. franchise? Yet
the honourable member for Westminster says that 7l.
is no great extension, and out of all comparison with
universal suffrage; so he excuses himself for having
thrown overboard all the safeguards which he has
recommended should be girt round universal suffrage.
I do not object to his throwing them overboard.
Checks and safeguards, in my opinion, generally
require other safeguards to take care of them. The
first use universal suffrage would make of its univer-
sality would be to throw the safeguards over altogether. He says the 7l. franchise has nothing to do
with safeguards. The Chancellor of the Exchequer
goes to universal suffrage, and the other two to whom
I have referred profess they go to household suffrage.
Do you think you could stop there? You talk of
touching ground—would it be solid ground or quick-
sand? You think that when you have got down to
that, you can create a sort of household aristocracy.
The thing is ridiculous. The working classes protest
even now against what they call a brick-and-mortar
suffrage. They say, "A man's a man for a' that."
The Bill appears to me to be the work of men who—

> " At once all law, all settlement control,
> And mend the parts by ruin of the whole.
> The tampering world is subject to this curse,
> To physic their disease into a worse."

What shall we gain by it? I have not, I think,
quibbled with the question. I have striven to do

what the Government have evaded doing—to extract
great principles out of this medley, (for medley it is,)
composed partly out of a veneration for numbers, and
partly out of a sort of traditional veneration for old
boroughs, which are to be preserved after what is
beneficial in them has been taken from them.   Then
we have to consider the proposed county franchise,
founded, as has been said, upon utter ignorance.   It
is quite evident that this Bill has been framed without information, because the Chancellor of the Exchequer, as is well known, has told us that the only
copy he had—I may be right; at any rate, I cannot
be wrong until I have stated it somehow.   The
Chancellor of the Exchequer told us that the only
copy he had of those statistics was the one that he
was obliged to lay on the table of the House.   If I
am wrong, let the right honourable gentleman contradict me.

The CHANCELLOR of the EXCHEQUER: I spoke of
the last absolutely finished copy.   The substance of
those statistics, as far as regarded the general bases
of the measure, had been in our hands for weeks
before that time, but was not in a state to be placed
on the table of the House until all the columns had
been filled in.

MR. LOWE: Well, Sir, that finished document is
what I call a copy.   It may be that the Bill was
originally drawn for 6*l.* and 12*l.*, and that at the last
moment 7*l.* and 14*l.* were substituted, and that it was

regarded as a matter of little consequence what the
exact figures were. As to the element of time, I
suppose, however, I must not say anything, or the
right honourable gentleman will be angry with me.
The twelve nights that he gave us for the Franchise
Bill are pretty well gone, and we have now got what
he never contemplated we should have, a Redistribution Bill as well. I suppose I had better say
nothing about the support the Government will have,
or I had better veil it in a dead language and say,
Idem trecenti juravimus. I would ask the Chancellor
of the Exchequer how he can expect to get the Bill
through committee under those circumstances, bear-
ing in mind that most of the newspapers that lay
claim to intelligence and write for educated persons,
having begun with rather vague notions of liberality,
have written themselves fairly out of them, and that
educated opinion is generally adverse to this measure.
These, Sir, are the prospects we have before us. We
have a measure of the most ill-considered and inade-
quate nature, which cannot be taken as it is, and which,
as I understand it, is based on principles so absolutely
subversive and destructive—the grouping, for instance
—that if we were ever so anxious to aid the Government, we could not accept it. Well then, Sir, what
objection can there be to the advice given to the
Government by my honourable friend, the member for
Dumfries—no hostile adviser—to put off the question
for another year, and give the educated opinion of

the country time to decide on this matter? What are the objections to such a course? There are only two, that I know of. One is, that honourable gentlemen are anxious, and very naturally anxious, for a settlement. But are there materials for a settlement in the Bill before us? How, for instance, can you settle the grouping? If you retain the principle on which the Government act, that of grouping those boroughs that have already members, you may do a little better than they have done, because they seem to have gone gratuitously wrong; but you cannot make an effective measure of it, and one that would stand. I am convinced it would generate far more discontent than it allayed, and create far more inequality than it seeks to remove. Then, the giving constituencies three members, is a principle of the greatest gravity and weight, not only for its actual results, but because it really concedes the principle of electoral districts. That, surely, is a matter not to be lightly disposed of; nor do I see how it can be compromised; because, if the Government gives it up, it must select some other apportionment, which can only be done by creating other electoral districts. Then, as regards the franchise; no doubt that we could get through, because it would only be dealing with a figure, and I dare say there are many honourable gentlemen whose opinions are entitled to great weight, who would like a compromise on the franchise. But then you have to consider this, that a compromise on

the franchise is a capitulation. Take what I said of
the opinions of the Chancellor of the Exchequer, the
honourable member for Birmingham, and the Attorney-General, and it is just as true of 8*l*. as of 7*l*.,
and of 9*l*. as of 8*l*. If you once give up the notion
of standing on the existing settlement, so far as the
mere money qualification for the franchise is concerned, whatever other qualifications you may add to
it, you give up the whole principle. As the Attorney-
General himself sees, you must go down to household
suffrage at last—whether any farther is a matter on
which men may differ, though, for my part, I think
you would have to go farther. I must say, therefore,
that I can see no materials for a compromise in the
borough franchise part of this Bill, and I come therefore to the conclusion that, desirable as it would be,
weary as we all are of the subject, and anxious as we
all are to get rid of it, there is no place for a compromise. The divergence is too wide, the principles
are too weighty, the time is too short, the information
is too defective, the subject is too ill-considered. Well,
then, the other objection to a postponement is that,
as my right honourable friend, the Secretary for the
Colonies, told us, the honour of the Government
would not permit them to take that course. Now,
I think we have heard too much about the honour of
the Government. The honour of the Government
obliged them to bring in a Reform Bill in 1860. It
was withdrawn under circumstances which I need not

allude to, and, as soon as it was withdrawn, the honour
of the Government went to sleep. It slept for five
years. Session after session it never so much as
winked. As long as Lord Palmerston lived, honour
slept soundly; but when Lord Palmerston died, and
Lord Russell succeeded by seniority to his place, the
" sleeping beauty" woke up. As long as the Government was kept together by having no Reform Bill,
honour did not ask for a Reform Bill; but when,
owing to the particular predilections of Lord Russell,
the Government was best kept together by having a
Reform Bill, honour became querulous and anxious
for a Reform Bill. But that, Sir, is a very peculiar
kind of honour. It puts me in mind of Hotspur's
description—

> " By Heaven, methinks it were an easy leap,
> To pluck bright honour from the pale-fac'd moon,
> Or dive into the bottom of the deep,
> Where fathom-line could never touch the ground,
> And pluck up drowned honour by the locks ;
> So he that doth redeem her thence might wear
> Without corrival all her dignities."

That is, as long as honour gives nothing, she is allowed
to sleep, and nobody cares about her; but when it is a
question of wearing " without corrival all her digni-
ties," honour becomes a most important and exacting
personage, and all considerations of policy and expediency have to be sacrificed to her imperious demands.
But then there is another difficulty. The Government have told us that they are bound in this matter.
Now, " bound " means contracted, and I want to

know with whom they contracted? Was it with the last House of Commons? But the plaintiff is dead, and has left no executor. Was it with the people at large? Well, wait till the people demand the fulfilment of the contract. But it was with neither the one nor the other, because the Under-Secretary for the Colonies let the cat out of the bag. He said that he himself called upon Earl Russell to redeem their pledge. I suppose he is Attorney-General for the people of England. He called upon the Government to redeem their pledge. Now, one often hears of people in insolvent circumstances, who want an excuse to become bankrupt, getting a friendly creditor to sue them. And this demand of the honourable gentleman has something of the same appearance. But there has been a little more honour in the case. The Government raised the banner in this House, and said they were determined we should pass the Franchise Bill without having seen the Redistribution Bill. Well, they carried their point, but carried it by that sort of majority, that, though they gained the victory, they scarcely got the honour of the operation, and if there was any doubt about that. I think there was no great accession of honour gained last Monday in the division, when the House really by their vote took the management of the Committee out of the hands of the Executive. All these things do not matter much to ordinary mortals, but to people of a Castilian turn of mind they are very serious. Sir, I have come to the conclusion that there must be two kinds of

honour, and the only consolation I can administer
to the Government is in the words of Hudibras—

> " If he that's in the battle slain
> He on the bed of honour lain,
> Then he that's beaten may be said
> To lie on honour's truckle bed.'

Well, Sir, as it seems to be the fashion to give the
Government advice. I will offer them a piece of
advice, and I will give them Falstaff's opinion of
honour—

> " What is honour? . . . a trim reckoning. . . . I'll none of it.
> Honour is a mere scutcheon, and so ends my catechism."

Sir, I am firmly convinced—and I wish, if possible,
to attract the serious attention of the House for a few
moments—that it is not the wish of this country to
do that which this Bill seeks to do   There is no
doubt the main object of this Bill is to render it impossible for any other Government than a Liberal
one to exist in this country for the future.   I do not
say that this object would appear an illegitimate one
in the eyes of heated partisans, and in moments of
conflict, for we are all of us naturally impatient of
opposition and contradiction, and I dare say such an
idea has occurred to many Governments before the
present, and to many Parliaments before this ; but I
do say that it is a short-sighted and foolish idea,
because, if we could succeed in utterly obliterating
and annihilating the power of honourable gentlemen
opposite, all we should reap as the reward of our
success would be the annihilation of ourselves.   The

history of this country—the glorious and happy
history of this country—has been a conflict between
two aristocratic parties, and if ever one should be
destroyed, the other would be left face to face with a
party not aristocratic, but purely democratic. The
honourable member for Birmingham said with great
truth the other day, that if the purely aristocratic
and the purely democratic elements should come into
conflict, the victory would, in all probability, be on the
side of Democracy. The annihilation of one of the
aristocratic parties—and I know it is in the minds of
many, though, of course, it is not openly avowed—
would be a folly like that of a bird which, feeling the
resistance the air offers to its flight, imagines how
well it would fly if there was no air at all, forgetting
that the very air which resists it also supports it,
and ministers to it the breath of life, and that if it
got quit of that air it would immediately perish. So
it is with political parties; they not only oppose, they
support, strengthen, and invigorate each other, and I
shall never, therefore, be a party to any measure,
come from whichever side of the House it may, which
seeks so to impair and destroy the balance of parties
existing in this country, that whichever party were in
office should be free from the check of a vigorous
opposition, directed by men of the same stamp and
position as those to whom they were opposed. I do
not believe that is an object of this Bill which the
people of this country will approve, nor do I believe
that they wish materially to diminish the influence

of honourable gentlemen opposite. There are plenty
of gentlemen who do wish it, but I do not believe it
is the wish of the country, and therefore I believe
they would have looked with much greater satisfaction on the principle of grouping, if it had not been
so studiously confined to represented boroughs, and if,
instead of first swamping the counties by a low franchise, and then offering the illusory boon of three
members, it had relieved the county constituencies of
considerable portions of the great towns by an efficient
Boundaries Bill, and had erected some of the towns
which now almost engross the county representation
into distinct constituencies. And while passing by that
point, let me say that the provisions with regard to
boundaries appear to me to be one of the most delusive
parts of the whole Bill, because the effect of them is that
no suburbs not now included in the municipal district
can be included in the Parliamentary district, unless
those who live in these suburbs are content to saddle
themselves with municipal taxation. I do not believe
the country wishes to see the door to talent shut more
closely than it is, or this House become an assembly
of millionaires. I do not believe the country would
look with satisfaction on the difference of tone within
the House which must be produced if the elements
of which it is the result are altered ; nor do I
believe that it will look with satisfaction on that
inevitable change of the Constitution which must
occur if these projects are carried into execution—
a change breaking the close connection between the

executive Government and the House of Commons.
I believe sincerely that this House is anxious to put
down corruption, and I will say again, at any risk of
obloquy, that it is not the way to put down corruption to thrust the franchise into poorer hands. If we
are really desirous of achieving this result, there is
but one way that I know of, and that is by taking
care that you trust the franchise only to those persons
whose position in life gives security that they are
above the grosser forms of corruption. And if you
do prefer to have a lower constituency, you must look
the thing in the face—you will be deliberately per-
petuating corruption for the sake of what you consider
the greater good of making the constituencies larger.
These are things which I do not believe the people
of this country wish to have. And, therefore, I
believe you will be acting in accordance with sound
wisdom and the enlightened public opinion of the
country by deferring this measure for another year.
I press most earnestly for delay. The matter is of
inexpressible importance; any error is absolutely
irretrievable; it is the last thing in the world which
ought to be dealt with rashly or incautiously. We
are dealing not merely with the administration, not
merely with a party—no, not even with the Constitution of the kingdom. To our hands at this moment
is intrusted the noble and sacred future of free and
self-determined government all over the world. We
are about to surrender certain good for more than
doubtful change; we are about to barter maxims and

traditions that have never failed, for theories and doctrines that never have succeeded. Democracy you may have at any time. Night and day the gate is open that leads to that bare and level plain, where every ant's nest is a mountain and every thistle a forest tree. But a Government such as England has, a Government the work of no human hand, but which has grown up the imperceptible aggregation of centuries—this is a thing which we only can enjoy, which we cannot impart to others, and which, once lost, we cannot recover for ourselves. Because you have contrived to be at once dilatory and hasty heretofore, that is no reason for pressing forward rashly and improvidently now. We are not agreed upon details, we have not come to any accord upon principles. To precipitate a decision in the case of a single human life would be cruel. It is more than cruel—it is parricide in the case of the Constitution, which is the life and soul of this great nation. If it is to perish, as all human things must perish, give it at any rate time to gather its robe about it, and to fall with decency and deliberation.

> " To-morrow !
> Oh that's sudden ! spare it ! spare it !
> It ought not so to die."

LONDON: PRINTED BY WILLIAM CLOWES AND SONS, STAMFORD STREET AND CHARING CROSS.

www.ingramcontent.com/pod-product-compliance
Lightning Source LLC
Chambersburg PA
CBHW030823270326
41928CB00007B/876